creative
textiles projects
for children

7 days
746 WOO

DS008572

CORNWALL COLLEGE

creative textiles projects
for children

Karen Woods

A & C Black • London

In memory of my mother, Sybil Woods,
who passed away before this book was finished.

First published in Great Britain in 2008
A & C Black Publishers Limited
38 Soho Square
London W1D 3HB
www.acblack.com

ISBN-13: 978-07136-8541-1

Copyright © 2008 Karen Woods

CIP Catalogue records for this book are available
from the British Library and the U.S. Library of
Congress.

All rights reserved. No part of this publication
may be reproduced in any form or by any means
– graphic, electronic, or mechanical, including
photocopying, recording, taping or information
storage and retrieval systems – without the prior
permission in writing of the publishers.

Karen Woods has asserted her right under the
Copyright, Design and Patents Act, 1988, to be
identified as the author of this work.

Typeset in 10 on 13pt Berkeley Book

Book design by Susan McIntyre
Cover design by Sutchinda Rangsi Thompson
Commissioning Editor: Susan James
Copyeditor: Julian Beecroft
Proofreader: Lucy Hawkes

Printed and bound in China

A & C Black uses paper produced with elemental
chlorine-free pulp, harvested from managed
sustainable forests.

contents

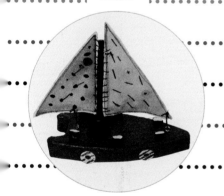

ACKNOWLEDGEMENTS ●

Thanks to everyone who made this book happen: Nic Barfield, for support and suggestions;
Chris Webb, for photography and patience; and the children who took part in the projects –
Obi and Noah Groombarke, Eartha Johnson, Connie Hobbs and Libby Wildbore. I'm also
grateful to Coats Crafts UK Ltd for kindly supplying hand-sewing threads.

introduction

ABOUT TEXTILES

Textiles are incredibly versatile. Ever since primitive humans worked out how to knot, knit, spin and weave, textiles have both clothed us and excited our senses. They can combine visual stimuli with the added bonuses of touch and smell. Their flexibility as a medium lies in their ability to fuse function and aesthetics. The ease with which they can be adapted for commercial use or individual creativity never ceases to amaze.

The term 'textiles' is vast, covering everything from the new generation of 'smart' hi-tech fibres for fashion, healthcare, sportswear and aerospace applications, to individual handmade artworks and more traditional artisan products such as prints, weaves, knits and embroideries.

Textile art is a stimulating medium for children. Even simple projects help to develop problem-solving, visualisation, planning and coordination skills. It also encourages children to focus on creativity by encouraging them to produce individual pieces that crystallise their inspiration and imagination.

ABOUT THIS BOOK

This book shows what children can create and achieve with no previous knowledge of textile skills and techniques. Its aim is to provide fun and a sense of achievement for the children, as well as empowering teachers/supervisors and parents by giving them the confidence to guide children through the projects successfully.

The book can be used in conjunction with the Key Stages 1 & 2 Art & Design Curriculum to build upon expressing ideas in colour, shape and texture, while encouraging and motivating the development of ideas.

Each project produces an artwork that can be either a stand-alone creation or incorporated into larger group-work projects for classrooms or public spaces. Each project also teaches and then reinforces structured ways of thinking, seeing, planning and making, to give a progression of learned outcomes.

Most of the projects require fairly basic equipment; the only specialist tool needed is an electric sewing machine. Most of the materials can be found in the home; the rest can be bought relatively cheaply from art, craft or DIY shops.

1 tiger head

This chapter shows how to use basic fabric-painting techniques. It encourages children to recognise shapes that they can combine to create more complex images. It introduces the idea of working through stages – drawing, outlining, filling in and adding details.

Children will learn to recognise the painterly effects of different brush sizes and how to improve brush control.

TECHNIQUES USED ....

✤ Preparing a work surface
✤ Selecting found objects for use as templates
✤ Tracing outline shapes
✤ Drawing freehand
✤ Filling in colour
✤ Ironing off
✤ Painting detail
✤ Cutting out

MATERIALS REQUIRED ......

✤ Plain fabric
✤ Pencils or fabric pens
✤ Fabric paints
✤ Iron and ironing board
✤ Variety of found objects for templates
✤ Scissors or shears

1 Ironing fabric

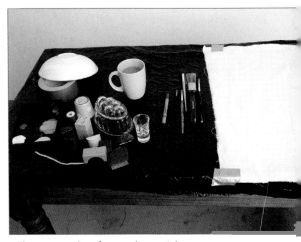

2 The prepared surface and materials

1 Your design can be traced onto any natural fabric – cotton and linen are best. Medium-weight calico is the easiest fabric to obtain and use, but old bed sheets, pillow-cases and tablecloths will work fine. Don't use nylon or synthetic materials as textile paint does not adhere to these surfaces.

Whatever material you do use, the best results will be obtained if you prepare a smooth surface by ironing out folds and wrinkles.

• •

2 Your work area needs to be flat and large enough to spread out your materials, tools and the fabric you'll be painting. Protect worktops with some plastic sheet taped to the work surface. A bin liner slit down one side with the bottom cut off will cover a large area.

3 Tracing around the basic template

Stretch the fabric tightly and tape the corners with duct tape – this keeps it smooth, stops it moving about and makes it easier to paint on.

• •

3 A medium-sized plate or cereal bowl is about the right size for the basic template of the tiger's head. Holding the plate or bowl firmly, trace around it with a fabric pen to produce a circular outline.

4 Building up the design (1)

4 Building up the design (2)

Building up the design (3)

5 Adding freehand detail

6 Painting the background colour

4 Pick out objects to build up different parts of the tiger's face – eyes, nose, chin, mouth, ears, etc. The chin was created using part of the outline of an oval jelly mould. A triangular building block was used as a template for the tiger's nose.

Try making different expressions using found objects. Shot glasses or eggcups are ideal for eyes. A line drawn across the eye will make your tiger look sleepy, with drooping eyelids!

It's surprising the number of household objects that can be used once you start looking hard at their shapes. A five-year-old recognised that this nit comb would make a perfect tiger's ear!

5 Children with well-developed drawing skills may want to draw freehand shapes. Here triangles of different sizes are being added to represent the ruffed-up fur around the tiger's face.

6 Fill in the background colour first using a medium-sized brush. Don't be afraid to use plenty of paint. Keeping the brush wet at all times makes the paint flow better on the fabric.

7 Putting shading over the background colour

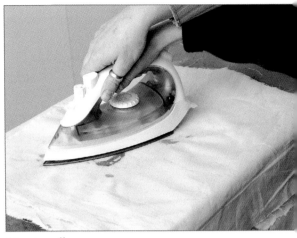

8 Ironing off

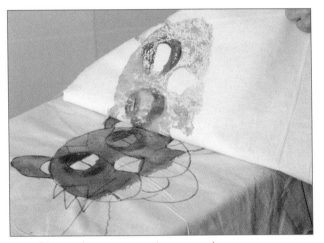

9 Dry fabric with any excess paint removed

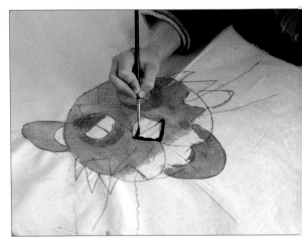

10 Outlining with a fine brush

7 While the background colour is still damp, different areas can be lightened or darkened to create shading, contrast and depth. It's best not to add details like nose, whiskers, etc. while the background fabric is wet, otherwise the colours will run into each other.

8 The beauty of fabric painting is that you don't have to wait for painted areas to dry. Simply put a piece of clean cloth over the work and iron off. Then you're ready to use different colours on top of the background without the paints bleeding into each other.

9 The heat and pressure of the iron fixes the colours on the fabric. Any excess paint is absorbed by the top piece of cloth. Peel this away, and the design is ready for you to add more colours.

10 When you're filling in small areas like the tiger's nose, outlining the shape first with a small brush will make the job neater and easier.

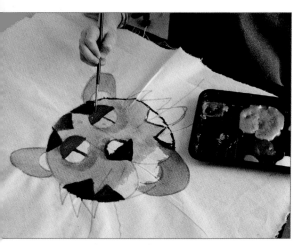

11 Developing the face

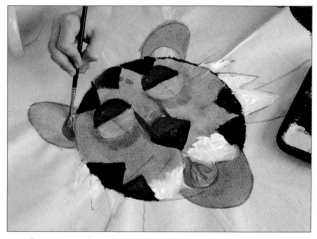

12 Filling in detail

13 The final touches

14 Cutting out

11 You can add detail and depth by using blended colours.

12 Don't forget that any colours can be mixed – like this bright pink for the tiger's tongue and the inside of his ears. Fabric paints are available in a wide range of colours, but it's cheaper to buy big bottles of basic primary colours plus black and white, then experiment with mixing different shades and tones.

13 Detail such as highlights, whiskers and spots are added freehand to complete the picture.

14 If you want to use the finished image as part of a larger picture (as in the jungle scene project later on in this book), you can cut the image out. Cutting out is best done with pinking shears. The zigzag cut stops the cut edges of the work from fraying.

2 leaves and flowers

This chapter simply takes the basic cutting, pasting and fabric-painting techniques learnt in the first workshop, and then goes a stage further. Heat-bonded adhesive is used, as well as textile glue. And stitch – both free-machine embroidery and hand-stitching – is added, together with decorative embellishments.

TECHNIQUES USED ....

✤ Fabric drawing and painting
✤ Sticking with heat-bonded adhesive
✤ Gluing
✤ Ironing off
✤ Stretching the fabric in the embroidery ring
✤ Free-machine embroidery
✤ Hand-stitching
✤ Beading

MATERIALS REQUIRED ....

✤ Plain fabric such as calico, cotton or lawn
✤ Fabric pens and crayons
✤ Fabric paints
✤ Heat-bonded adhesive
✤ Hand and machine threads
✤ Textile glue
✤ Beads or buttons

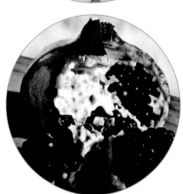

Choose big, bright images of fruit, flowers and leaves from books, magazines and the internet – gardening and food magazines are a great place to start. Alternatively, you can simply draw fruit or leaves from life – take inspiration from a walk in the country, a stroll through the fresh-produce section of the supermarket, or even the fruit bowl at home.

1 Drawing a flower shape   2 Filling in the design   3 Ironing off

1 Using a piece of plain natural fabric – an old cotton sheet or pillowcase is fine – draw a flower shape using fabric crayons or pens

2 Use textile paints to fill in and decorate the flower. If you want to blend colours, that's fine – but remember to iron off the separate colours if you want to stop them running together.

3 When you have finished painting the flower, place a clean piece of scrap fabric over the design and iron it to dry and fix the paint.

4 Turn the flower over and cut a piece of heat-bonded web adhesive big enough to cover the design. Place the web with the rough side directly against the back of the fabric. The protective paper should be facing upwards.

Iron over the protective backing paper to bond the web to the back of the fabric.

5 With small scissors, cut carefully around the edges of the flower.

4 Placing heat-bonded web on the back of the design

5 Cutting out the flower

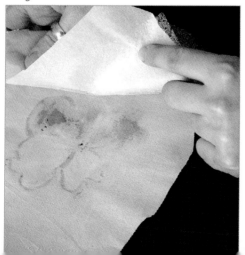

6 Peeling off the protective backing paper

7 Covering work with clean fabric

8 Cutting the background to shape with pinking shears

6 Carefully peel off the protective backing paper, exposing the adhesive surface on the back of the flower. When this is heat-bonded using an iron, it will stick the flower to a piece of backing fabric without using pins or messy glue. Heat-bonded adhesive also gives a smooth finish that is easy to work with.

7 Position the bonded flower onto a background fabric (here we have used felt). Then place a clean piece of scrap cloth over the work, and iron off to fix into position.

> ### TOP TIP
> *Placing a piece of fabric on top of the work protects against marking and scorching.*

8 On this flower, we have used pinking shears to give a decorative edge, cutting around to follow the line of our original flower design. Edges can be frayed, pinked and cut away, and extra layers of backing fabric can be added to give more depth, weight and contrast. (See the workshop on flower brooches to develop these techniques further.)

9 Tie a knot at the end of a piece of hand-sewing thread. The knot needs to be big enough to prevent the thread being pulled through the fabric.

9 Knotting the end of a piece of hand-sewing thread

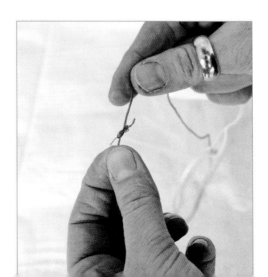

Start at the back of the flower, near the middle. Holding the needle at the eye end, carefully push it through the fabric. When the point of the needle comes through the fabric, hold the needle with the index finger and thumb as far down from the point as possible. Then wiggle the needle until the whole needle has come through the fabric. Then grip the thread against the eye of the needle with index finger and thumb, gently pulling through all the thread.

10 Thread as many beads, sequins or buttons as you like. Secure each bead you add by stitching through to the back of the work, then coming back to the front side. Repeat this process until all the decorations are securely attached.

Finish the hand-sewing with two or three stitches on top of each other, or tie a knot from the ends of the threads.

10 Threading a bead

11 Draw leaf shapes using fabric pens or crayons, and then fill in with fabric paint. As with the flower, you can blend colours or keep them distinct and separate. Here we have chosen to use a lighter colour on top of the leaf green to highlight the tones.

Iron off to fix and dry the paint.

Details such as veins and patterning can be created on the leaf by adding them with fabric pens and paints. Or you can print or stencil – see the Jungle scene Workshop for tips on these techniques.

12 Here we have used thin strips of silver fabric treated with heat-bonded adhesive so that they can be stuck to the surface of the leaf. They really stand out well – this sort of appliqué is worth the extra effort and can be adapted to many different projects.

11 Drawing and filling in leaf shapes (1)

Drawing and filling in leaf shapes (2)

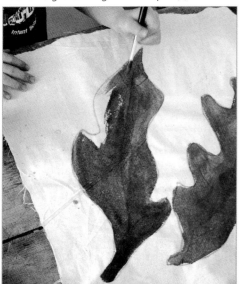

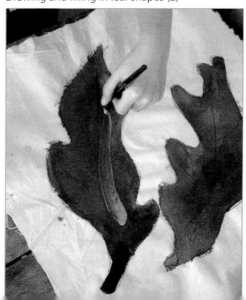

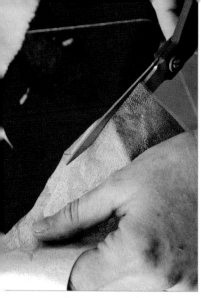

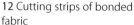

12 Cutting strips of bonded fabric

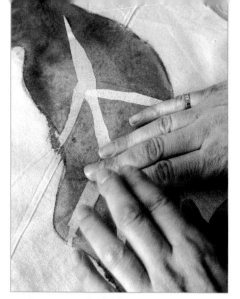

13 Positioning the leaf veins on the leaf

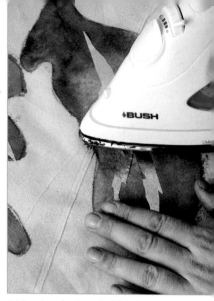

14 Ironing the bonded fabric into place

Iron a piece of heat-bonded adhesive web onto the back of the decorative fabric. You can draw patterns, shapes and templates onto the protective backing paper as a guide before you cut up the fabric. Here we are simply cutting freehand to make strips for the leaf veins.

. . . .

13 Peel off the protective backing paper and place the leaf veins bonded side down onto the surface of the leaf.

. . . .

14 With a clean iron on a cool setting, very carefully iron the thin strips onto the leaf to fix them. We are not using a covering cloth here, because the thin fabric strips are very fiddly and we want to see that they stay in the desired position as we iron them on.

. . . .

15 Putting your work into an embroidery ring stretches the fabric tight, preventing the cloth from puckering or moving. Using the ring also makes it much easier for children to move and control the work when doing free-machine stitching.

Using a free-machine foot or darning foot, and with the teeth dropped or covered, set the stitch width to 0 or straight stitch. Lift the presser foot at the back of the machine – this lever lifts the foot up and down. Slide the ring with the work secured to the machine's table or 'bed'. Then put the presser foot back down.

You are now ready to do some free-machine embroidery.

15 Placing the work in an embroidery ring

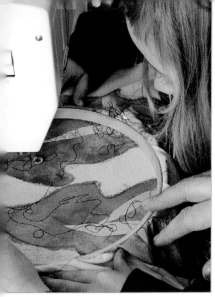

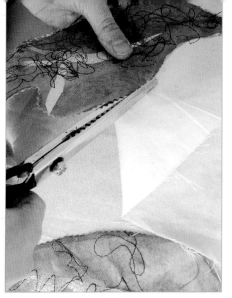

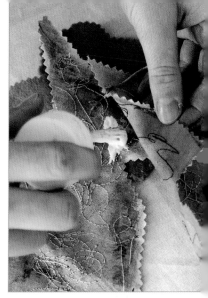

16 Adding decorative stitching   **17** Cutting out the leaf shape   **18** Gluing the leaves to the flower

16 Make sure the child's hands are always on the outside of the embroidery ring. Using gentle guidance, help the child to slowly move the ring around the needle to create a free stitch.

To begin with, you might find it easier if you control the speed of the machine with the foot pedal, leaving the child free to concentrate on the stitching. Even older children will find they need a bit of practice to master the coordination of controlling the speed while moving the ring smoothly to build up a design.

17 When your stitched decoration is complete, take the work out of the embroidery ring. Then cut around the leaf shape. Pinking shears can be used to give a realistically jagged, leaf-like appearance to the edge.

18 Here the two leaves have been attached to the flower with a couple of big stitches, just to give them a bit of extra strength. Textile glue or PVA can be used to hold all the pieces together. Press firmly together and allow to dry.

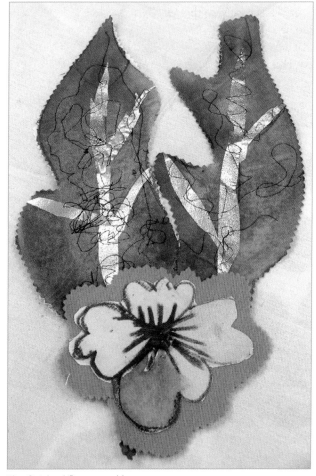

The finished flower and leaves

3 jungle scene

This chapter takes the basic technique of fabric painting from the first workshop and adds printing, stencilling and other types of mark-making plus collage to create a jungle scene.

Working on a large scene allows this project to be adapted for bigger groups. Separate elements can be prepared by individuals or small work groups, with all the parts being brought together to create a collaborative work.

Tiger heads created in the first workshop have been added to the jungle scene. Other creatures can also be incorporated. And when further skills and techniques have been acquired, objects such as fruit and flowers can be created to enhance the scene. Three-dimensional items such as flower brooches and teabag flowers (see separate projects) can be added to give extra texture and depth.

TECHNIQUES USED

❖ Fabric painting and drawing
❖ Printing and stencilling with found objects
❖ Cutting stencils
❖ Creating printing blocks
❖ Cutting
❖ Gluing

MATERIALS REQUIRED

❖ Plain natural fabric – an old bed sheet, tablecloth or piece of calico
❖ Fabric paints
❖ Fabric crayons and marker pens
❖ Fruit and vegetables – apple, orange, lemon, potato, carrot, pumpkin
❖ Thin card (for stencils)
❖ Thick cardboard (for printing blocks)
❖ Empty cotton bobbins
❖ Cooking utensils – spatula, slotted spoon, potato masher
❖ Plastic bubble wrap
❖ Thin textured rubber or plastic sheet/mat
❖ Beads, buttons, washers, screw-fixing plugs, matchsticks, pasta
❖ PVA adhesive
❖ Thin sticks or willow/hazel rods

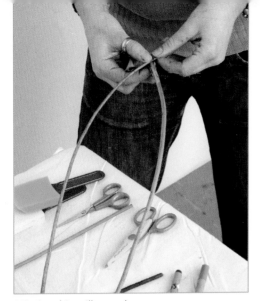

1 Taping thin willow rods

Iron the large piece of cloth for your jungle background and tape it to a flat surface.

Plan the layout loosely – where do you want your trees, leaves and fruit? Where are you going to put the animals you choose to live in your jungle?

1 Draw a rough design with fabric pens. If you want to create smooth curves for tree trunks and leaves, you can make a basic shape with two pieces of thin wood. Tape the two pieces firmly together at one end, then the other two ends can be adjusted to form thinner or fatter leaf shapes.

2 A single piece of thin willow/hazel rod or a garden stick can be used as a curved rule or guide.

3 Fill in the basic outline shapes with fabric paints. Experiment with mixing different colours when they are wet to create tones and highlights.

Using rods to create leaf shapes

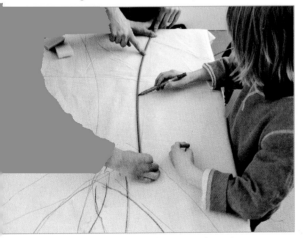

2 Using a garden stick as a guide to draw a treetrunk

3 Painting the leaves and trunk

  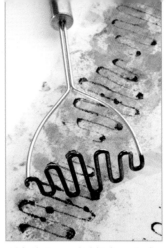 

4 LEFT TO RIGHT A section of mountain-bike tyre used as a printing block; an apple block made from a cut-up hot-water bottle; potato masher as printing tool; bubble wrap as a printing tool.

Leave the work to dry while you make your printing blocks and stencils. Alternatively, if you want to get on with your design, simply iron off the work to dry and fix the paint, like you did with the tiger's head in the first workshop.

. . . .

4 There are lots of ways to make marks that give interesting shapes, patterns and textures. Two basic techniques are printing and stencilling, and both are very versatile and adaptable, using familiar objects in new ways.

Printing uses paint or ink on the surface of an object. The object is pressed onto the surface of your work, leaving some of the ink or paint behind and transferring the shape of the object.

The most basic form of printing uses your own body – thumbs, fingers, hands, feet – to make simple marks. We have used some finger and thumb prints in our jungle scene – just like our primitive ancestors did on the walls of their caves thousands of years ago.

Most forms of printing need a block, an object that is easy to handle and that carries a surface shape or pattern that will be transferred when it is covered with ink or paint.

Empty cotton bobbins, empty matchboxes and wooden building blocks all make excellent bases for printing blocks because they are easy to grip. Shapes can be cut out of all sorts of material and stuck to the bobbin, box or block. Look for materials with lots of surface texture or interesting designs and patterns – lines, curves, circles.

. . . .

Some found objects create interesting patterns. Above you can see the squiggly pattern left by a potato masher. Other kitchen items include the prongs of a fork, the back of a spoon, the rims of eggcups and cups or glasses of different sizes, pan scourers, dish brushes and scrubbing brushes, small sponges… Take a look in the bathroom, too – toothbrushes and combs can make interesting printing tools.

. . . .

Plastic bubble wrap has a great texture for printing. Corrugated cardboard is good, too. So are some polystyrene packing materials. See what you can find around the house!

jungle scene

4 LEFT TO RIGHT A Lego brick makes a simple printing block; thin foam plastic sheet; matchsticks stuck to a card base, resembling the veins on a leaf.

Other found objects could be in your toy box. Here we've used a Lego brick. You can print from the top, bottom or even sides of building blocks like this – they will all give different patterns. Wheels off broken toys also make some great shapes.

••••••••••••••••••••••••••••••••

Thin foam plastic sheet is easy to cut and mark. Here we have cut through to create a geometric shape which we're going to use to represent a pineapple for our jungle.

Small regular-sized objects can be stuck to a piece of card coated with PVA glue. The objects can be arranged and grouped together to create patterns like the veins on a leaf.

••••••••••••••••••••••••••••••••

If you arrange objects in certain formations, the block can be moved to create repeat patterns. This printing block made from screw-fixing plugs can be printed end to end to give the effect of bark on a tree trunk.

••••••••••••••••••••••••••••••••

Buttons, coins, washers, dried pasta shapes (thin tubes and smaller shapes are best) and

LEFT TO RIGHT Screw-fixing plugs forming a bark pattern; buttons of different sizes and patterns; small beads give a delicate repeat pattern.

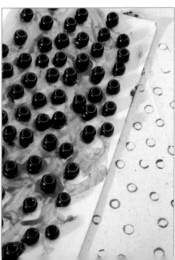

LEFT TO RIGHT Leaves created from a cut-up hot-water bottle; fruit prints; the end of a butternut squash.

beads can all be embedded in a thick layer of PVA. Leave to dry overnight.

Cutting shapes out of interestingly textured materials and sticking them to a backing block or card can create more complex designs. Here we've used scraps of cut-up hot-water bottle to create multiple palm-like leaves.

Most firm fruits and vegetables can be cut in half to produce beautiful ready-made shapes for printing. Some – like apples and oranges

– just need cutting in half neatly. Others can be sliced – aubergines and butternut squash are good for this. Larger fruits or vegetables can be cut into slices or sections – try cutting a piece off a tight white cabbage, a head of broccoli or a slice of pumpkin or unripe melon!

A classic way of making a printed mark is to use a potato block (other hard vegetables such as turnips and swedes work just as well). You need to use a sharp knife – so get an adult to help. Experiment with different ways of cutting into the potato.

LEFT TO RIGHT A slice of pumpkin; potato prints.

  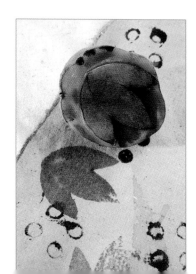

5 LEFT TO RIGHT A frying slice can be used as a stencil; a slotted spoon being used as a stencil; repeat stencil patterns cut into a piece of card.

5 The second major textile mark-making technique is stencilling, where paint or ink is forced through the spaces in an object to leave a pattern on the cloth.

You can cut stencils from almost any stiff, non-absorbent material. Thin card and flexible plastic sheet such as acetate are easiest to work with, but heavyweight plastic sacks, foam plastic sheet and cardboard can all be used if you want to create really big stencil designs. Again, household objects can be used as stencils.

Adult help may be needed to cut stencils – smaller designs are more easily cut with a craft knife than with scissors.

When using your stencils, it's easiest to tape the stencil down to the piece you are making and then to work paint into the stencil with a sponge or medium brush. Experiment with adding different colours or tones.

When you have applied paint, carefully remove the tape from the stencil and lift it straight off without dragging it across the painted surface.

6 The images on your jungle scene can be built up with different textures and colours using different types of printing blocks and stencils.

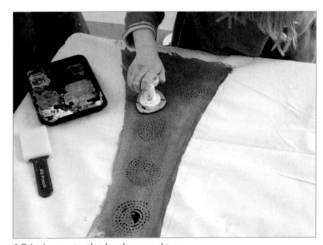

6 Printing onto the background tree

7 We've printed marks on the tree trunk, and now we're adding extra leaves and foliage drawn freehand. This will form part of the jungle undergrowth where our animals will hide.

Use your imagination and a variety of tools and techniques to give the scene all the depth and mystery that a real jungle would have.

7 Adding freehand leaf shapes

8 As well as painting some more leaves, we decided to add cut-out creatures like the tiger from the first workshop. We also used printing techniques on plain fabric, then cut these into leaf and grass shapes. These can be stuck onto the jungle background to give more depth.

Using a leaf guide

Filling in leaf detail

8 Gluing the tiger to the jungle scene

9 Gluing cut-out leaf shapes (1)

Gluing cut-out leaf shapes (2)

10 Using a large cut-card stencil to create grass (1)

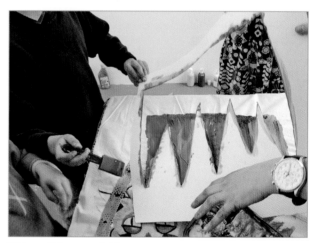

Lifting off the stencil (2)

11 Filling in to combine all the elements

9 The printed leaves and blades of jungle grass can be glued so that they overlap the tiger's head and background.

10 We used a card stencil to create big bold blades of jungle grass at the bottom of the jungle scene.

11 To complete the feel of a dark, mysterious jungle, you really need to fill in any gaps. We've used a mixture of rich dark colours – browns, gold and black – to join up all the different parts of the picture.

12 Added detail: printing pineapple shapes (1)

Added detail: printing pineapple shapes (2)

13 Apple printing block (1)

Apple prints (2)

This draws the eye to the brighter elements of the picture such as the leaves and the tiger's eyes.

....

12 We decided that our jungle needed some fruit on the trees. Here we've made a pineapple shape from a cut-out foam plastic sheet.

....

13 And then we added more fruit – apples! We used an apple printing block made of a cut-up hot-water bottle. And then we used the real thing, cut in half.

Apple prints using a cut apple (3)

14 Leaf texture using a beaded printing block (1)

Leaf texture using a beaded printing block (2)

14 The big leaves in the scene were given extra texture by overprinting them with a printing block made with small plastic beads.

15 Finally we added highlights to the tree trunks by simply dipping a finger in white paint.

15 Back to basics: finger-painting

4 flower brooches

This chapter shows how layering of cut-outs in fabrics and other media can produce three-dimensional effects and contrasts.

TECHNIQUES USED ··············

❖ Making templates
❖ Fabric cutting
❖ Sticking and attaching
❖ Decorating, beadwork

MATERIALS REQUIRED ··········

❖ Scrap fabrics
❖ Hand-sewing threads
❖ Beads
❖ Buttons
❖ Washers
❖ Flower or cake decorations
❖ PVA or craft glue
❖ Brooch fastenings or safety pins

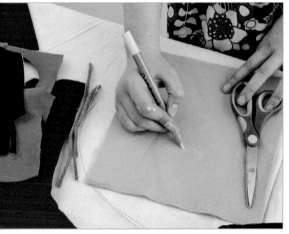

1 Drawing shapes
2 Cutting out

1 Draw simple flower shapes on the fabric scraps. These can be freehand drawings, or you can use real flowers or found objects to create your own shapes.

You will need several layers to create your brooch. It's best to start with a large shape on the bottom layer and build up with smaller shapes for the middle and top layers.

2 Cut round the lines you've drawn. Remember to turn the work, not the scissors, as you cut round the shape.

You can create a variety of edges for effect and texture. Try pinking, fraying and fringing different weights and textures of fabric.

 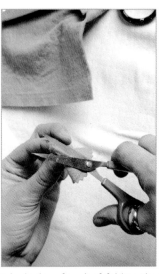 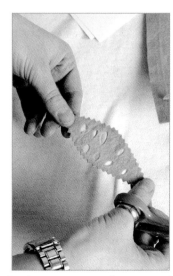 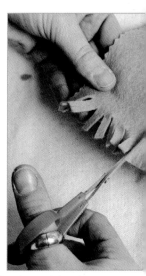

2 LEFT TO RIGHT Cutting pinked edges for a leaf; folding the leaf and cutting out small sections; a leaf with cut-through patterns; cutting a fringed edge.

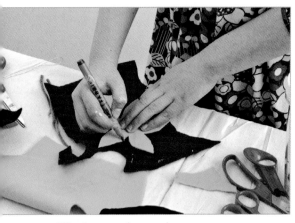

3 Tracing round a template
4 Positioning the various layers

3 A quick way of making repeat or multiple objects is to trace round an original shape or drawing. This is called a template.

4 Make several flower shapes in different sizes using a variety of materials.

Position the cutwork carefully on a flat surface, arranging each layer to give the best effect. Remember that the upper layers need to be smaller than the lower ones!

You can add quirky found objects, too. Try mixing realistic-looking leaves from plastic flower arrangements, cake decorations or wedding bouquets. Alternatively, you can use plastic sheets, acetates, felts, thin rubber, cut-up polystyrene cups, coloured cardboard or even thick paper to vary the look and texture of your brooches.

5 Thread a large-eyed needle (the sharper the better, because you're stitching through lots of layers). Put a knot at the end of some hand-sewing thread rather than close to the eye of the needle.

Pick up the arrangement of flower layers (and optional leaves), holding it tightly between finger and thumb. (Younger children may need an adult to hold the work and, initially, to show them how to push the needle through the layers from the bottom, and then back through from the front.) Repeat the stitching (back to front and front to back) several times to hold the layers firmly together.

5 Sewing through to attach the layers

6 To ensure your layers stay firmly in place, either tie several knots close to the back of the fabric, or put two little stitches on top of each other. Then cut the thread.

7 For added depth and stronger three-dimensional effects, try sandwiching buttons, beads or washers between the layers.

6 Tying off stitches

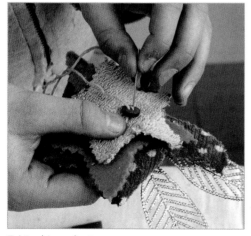

7 Attaching a button

Sandwiching a button between layers

33

8 Tracing a disc template

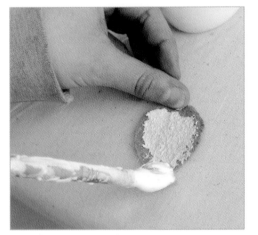

9 Gluing the backing disc

8 To make a neat backing for your brooch, trace a circle onto felt or some other fabric that won't tear or fray.

9 Cover one side of the backing disc with PVA or craft glue.

10 Firmly press the backing disc over the stitching and knots on the back of the brooch. This keeps everything together and will provide a flat surface onto which you can stitch your brooch fastener.

11 Using thick hand-sewing thread, stitch through each hole of the brooch fastening into the backing disc. Try to catch just the fabric of the bottom layer – not all the layers.

You can buy brooch fastenings at craft and haberdashery shops, or you can use safety pins as a cheap alternative.

10 Sticking the backing disc to the back of the brooch

11 Attaching a brooch fastening

12 This brooch uses a bottom layer of pink felt, followed by a layer of towelling, then lilac silk and finally more felt. The edges are pinked, with the top layer pinked and cut into to give a frond effect. Added decoration is provided by a silver leaf from a flower-arranging kit and a diamante bead.

13 This brooch was created using three layers of felt cut into different shapes, backed with a towelling leaf and finished with a plastic 'pop art' button.

12 A finished example of a flower brooch

13 A very simple brooch

14 When you really want to embellish, the end result can be as lavish as this brooch. The bottom layer is pinked and fronded felt, topped by hand-painted calico and backed by a patterned leaf. Decoration includes plastic beads, sequins, washers, nuts and tiny bells. Hand-stitching with different threads has been used to gather, or ruche, the top layer to give even more texture.

14 Everything but the kitchen sink!

5 teabag flowers

This chapter is a quick and very accessible workshop. The end product can be a single flower, a garland or bouquet, or decorative brooches and fashion accessories.

It can also be developed for older children or classes to produce different types of teabag objects as one aspect of a larger project. The teabags are versatile – instead of being glued and stitched as in this flower project, they can be hung from wire or string, made into mobiles, stuck onto windows, or even fixed together to form larger artworks.

Images, words and symbols can be inserted in the teabags, making them ideal for use within other studies – for example, inserting maps into a geography wall display, or dried flowers and leaves into a natural-science project.

TECHNIQUES USED ....

✤ Cutting
✤ Latex dipping
✤ Painting
✤ Machine- and hand-stitching
✤ Decorative embellishment
✤ Attaching
✤ Wiring

MATERIALS REQUIRED ....

✤ Teabags (round ones are best)
✤ Small two-dimensional objects for inserting
✤ Liquid latex
✤ Acrylic paints
✤ Thin garden cane
✤ Pipe cleaners
✤ Felt or fabric
✤ PVA glue
✤ Hand and machine thread

1 Choose suitable images and objects that you can use to fill the teabags. Small flat objects such as sequins, stars, tiddlywinks, thin buttons and washers will all work well. Paper cut-outs – from books, magazines or your own drawings – are great, or look for readymade paper objects such as stamps, playing cards and photographs.

· ·

2 Pour enough liquid latex into a container to cover the bottom to a depth of about 1 cm (⅜ in.). The latex is safe to use but has an unpleasant smell, so you might want to work with the window open!

· ·

3 Add a small amount of pale paint to the latex. It's important to use a light shade – for example, a pearlescent white with just a hint of colour – because then the object or image in the teabag will show through. Alternatively, you can mix in a sprinkling of metallic glitter.

We will use this pale paint/latex mixture for all the teabags that contain objects or images. Other teabags without contents can be coloured more brightly by mixing in stronger shades.

1 Objects to fill teabags

4 Carefully cut along the edge of the teabag, rounding it off so that you keep the shape roughly circular. You only need to cut away enough of the edge to insert your chosen object or image.

Pour out the tea – if you put the loose tea into a clean container, it can still be used.

2 Pouring liquid latex into a container

3 Mixing colour into the latex

4 Cutting off the edge of a teabag

5 Shaping an image to fit the teabag

6 Putting an object into the teabag

7 Painting latex onto a teabag

5 Cut and shape your chosen images to fit into the teabags.

6 Put your objects and images into each teabag in turn. You might want to insert a single large image like this £500 Monopoly banknote, or a selection of smaller items such as shiny plastic-foil stars and shapes.

7 The liquid latex can be painted onto both sides of the teabag, or you can dip the teabag into the container of latex. Don't cover it too thickly – the thinner the coating, the better it works. With a brush, wipe off any excess latex over the container.

> ## TOP TIP
> *So that you don't waste latex, it's a good idea to cover all the teabags you need in pale colours first. Then you can add darker colours to the mixture you've already used.*

8 Teabag 'petals' that don't contain objects or images can be dipped or painted in strongly coloured latex. Experiment to get the shades you want.

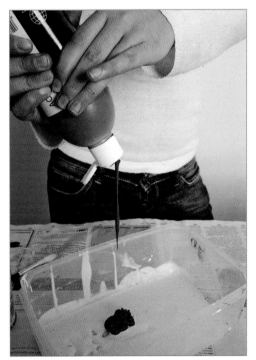

8 Adding darker colours

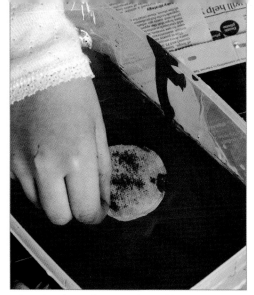

9 Dipping the teabag in coloured latex

10 Drying off the latex-covered teabags

9 Again, paint the latex thinly onto the teabag, or dip it in the coloured latex.

10 Hang the latex-covered teabags out to dry on a clothes line. Try to keep the clothes pegs as close to the edge of each teabag as possible, as they tend to mark the wet latex. Alternatively, you can use paper clips to hang up the bags. Leave to dry for at least a couple of hours – preferably longer.

11 Put a dab of PVA glue on the overlapping area of each teabag petal – it helps to lay out the petals on a flat surface first, so

that you can see where you need to glue. If there are any marks or tears from where the clothes pegs or clips have been, you can cover these with an overlapping petal.

12 Spread PVA glue thinly onto the back of the teabag that will form the centre of your flower.

13 Place the centre of the flower over the outer petals and press firmly. Then put the completed flower onto a plastic sheet (a plastic bag is fine) so that it doesn't stick to your work surface when it dries!

11 Arranging teabag petals to form a flower

12 Gluing the centre of the flower

13 Gluing the centre in place

14 Using a petal as a template for a fabric overlay

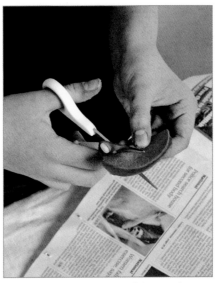

15 Cutting out the centre of the overlay to create a fabric ring

16 Gluing the overlay ring

14 You can use fabric or coloured paper/card to further decorate your flowers. Here we are using a teabag petal as a template to cut a felt overlay. Feel free to experiment with different types of effect – frills, fronds, pinked edges or whatever you fancy.

15 Fold the circle of fabric or card in half, then cut out the centre to leave an outer ring.

16 Paint a thin layer of PVA glue onto one side of the fabric/card overlay. Then position the overlay ring carefully over the centre of the flower, press down firmly and allow to dry. To speed up the process, you can iron it dry – but remember to place a piece of scrap fabric over the top of your flower.

17 With the machine set to straight stitch and the free-machine-embroidery foot on, use stitching to work patterns into the flower.

18 Use hand-stitching to add small objects such as pompoms, beads, buttons, sequins, etc. to give extra decorative detail.

19 If you want to display your flower in a pot, it will need a stalk. We have used a short piece of thin garden cane, but straws, thin dowel, plastic rods, thick wire and lollipop sticks will all do the job. Use strong tape to attach the stalk to the back of the flower.

17 Using stitch to decorate the flower

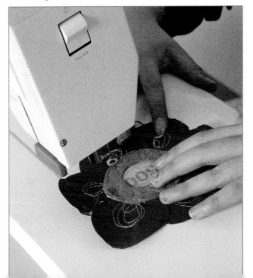

18 Stitching pompoms to the flower

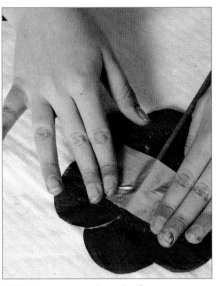

19 Fixing a cane stalk to the flower

20 Cutting the leaf shape

20 If you choose to put them on stalks, your flowers might look better with some leaves. Cut the shape of the leaf in card or fabric.

21 Use the cut leaf as a template to create exact copies that can be stitched together.

22 To create the veins and ribs on the leaves, try cutting thin strips of fabric and sticking them to the leaf. It is easiest to use pre-bonded fabric. Iron heat-bonded web onto the fabric with the paper layer facing upwards and the rough, glued side facing the back of the fabric. Alternatively, you can use craft glue or PVA – but spread it on very carefully and thinly.

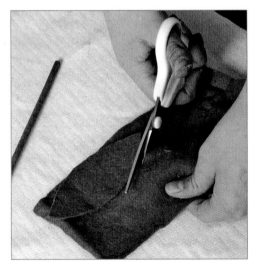

21 Using the cut leaf as a template

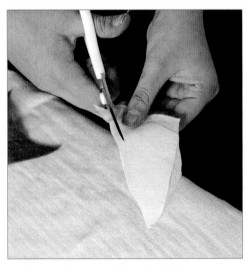

22 Cutting thin strips of bonded fabric

23 Peel off the paper backing from the bonded fabric strips

23 Removing the paper backing from the bonded fabric

24 Use an iron to heat-set the veins and ribs to the leaf. Fabric such as felt will stand a fairly high heat, but thin, delicate fabrics need to have a cloth placed over the work to protect them.

25 So that you can attach the leaf to the flower stalk, a pipe cleaner can be inserted between two layers of leaf. Either glue or stitch the two sides together, firmly securing the pipe cleaner in the middle.

26 Here we have set the machine to a small zigzag and sewn around the edge of the leaf, then up through the centre rib and along the veins. This is both functional – it holds the pipe cleaner in place – and decorative.

Attach the leaf to the stalk by twisting the pipe cleaner tightly around the stalk. The pipe cleaner through the leaf allows the leaf to be arranged and adjusted as you like.

24 Ironing the fabric strips onto the leaf

25 Laying the leaf sides together with a pipe cleaner

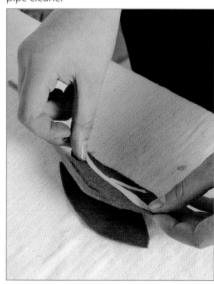

26 Adding functional and decorative stitching

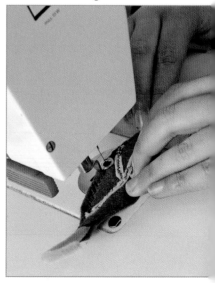

27 To show off our teabag flowers, we created this simple window display. Displays like this are easy to make and are very adaptable.

Take a shallow cardboard box for the window shape. Add thin strips of wood or cut-up bits of polystyrene packaging around the edges to make the frame, sill and window bars. Stick it all together with strong tape, then cover the whole structure with several layers of papier mâché (strips of newspaper glued with PVA). When this is dry, prime it with white emulsion paint. Allow to dry, then paint the window surrounds and window bars in the colours of your choice

The scene through the window panes can be created using photos, magazine pictures, your own paintings or drawings, or any mixture of these. Trim these carefully to size and stick down with PVA glue.

We made the curtains from scraps of printed fabric. We turned the tops of the curtains down about 2 cm (¾ in.), stitched along the edge and formed a tube into which we pushed a garden cane. Then we taped both ends of the cane to the top of the window. The curtain tie-backs are short pieces of ribbon tied back to tiny 'eye' screws.

The pelmet was made by cutting two strips of fabric to the desired depth and shape, putting the two 'right' sides together, then pinning and sewing them together. We left the top straight edge unsewn so that the piece could be turned through. Then we turned in the rough top edges and sewed them. Finally, we attached the pelmet to the sides of the box with glue.

27 An arrangement of teabag flowers in a window display

6 crazy creatures

This is a fun workshop that allows children to look at different body shapes, plan the different stages of making body parts, and then think about the whole picture – how the parts fit together, and how many ways they can be changed. The results can be humorous, bizarre and very silly – but they encourage children to be aware of what they actually see.

The techniques used have all been covered in previous workshops, but this workshop can go where the children want to take it – mixing and matching real animals with fantasy creations, humans with space aliens, prehistoric creatures with mythical monsters...

The wider the choice of body parts you produce, the bigger the range of creatures that can be created. This workshop is ideal for a class project, with each child contributing one or two body parts; these can be placed on a painted backdrop chosen to reflect whatever themes are topical in the classroom.

TECHNIQUES USED ....

❖ Making templates
❖ Cutting
❖ Fabric painting
❖ Sticking with iron-on web adhesive (Bondaweb)
❖ Machine- and hand-sewing
❖ Decoration with buttons, beads, etc.

MATERIALS REQUIRED ....

❖ Cardboard
❖ Plain fabric or calico
❖ Selection of different fabrics – felts, plastics, chiffons, papers, etc.
❖ Pencils or fabric pens
❖ Fabric paints
❖ Beads, buttons
❖ Hand-sewing threads, wools
❖ Gaffer tape or duct tape

1 Design and draw simple body parts as templates. To the left are the legs for a small dog. Use stiff card or thin cardboard – cereal packets are ideal.

1 Drawing body parts

2 Cutting out template shapes

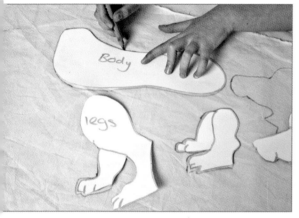

3 Drawing around template shapes

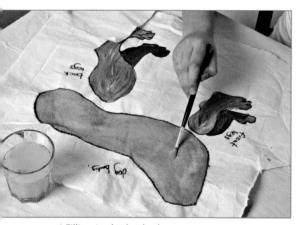

4 Filling in the body shapes
5 Ironing off

TOP TIP

It helps to have reference images so that children can identify which parts go to make up the whole creature: head, legs, arms, body/torso, feet, tail, etc.

2 Carefully cut out the template shapes for each body part.

3 Using duct tape, attach a piece of plain calico or an old bed sheet or pillowcase to the work surface. Then trace round each template shape with a fabric pen. Leave a generous border round each body part – this makes it easier to paint them and cut them out.

4 Using fabric paints, fill in each body part with background colours. You can blend colours together and use tones to create depth and detail. If you want to add further detail, remember to iron off after filling in the background colours, thus preventing the added detail from bleeding into the same background colours.

Detail can be added with a fine brush or with fabric pens and crayons.

5 Always iron off between stages – this dries the paint and fixes it, allowing you to add further colours or detail.

6 You can use appliqué to add detail and contrast to body parts. Here scraps of spotted fabric are being used. Use heat-fixed web adhesive (Bondaweb) to stick them to the dog's body parts. The heat-fixed adhesive is ironed onto the back of the spotted fabric, with the webbing side face down and the backing paper upwards.

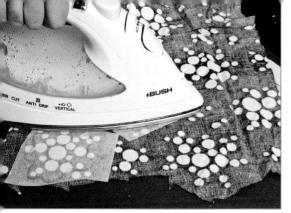

6 Applying heat-fixed web adhesive to the back of the fabric

7 Peeling away the paper backing

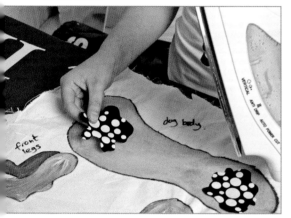

8 Positioning appliqué patches on body parts

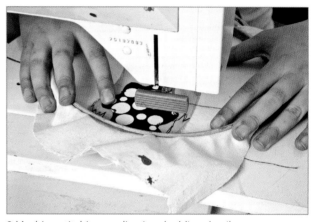

9 Machine-stitching appliqué and adding detail

Designs for the decorative appliqué patches can be drawn with a pen onto the paper backing.

. . . .

7 Cut neatly around the outline of the appliqué shape, then peel off the paper backing.

. . . .

8 Place the appliqué patches where you want them. Then carefully put a clean cloth over the top and iron them to fix. This holds the patches firmly in place so that you can stitch them.

. . . .

9 Put the work into an embroidery ring. Set the machine to zigzag stitch. Keep as close to the edge of the patch as possible and stitch around the shape. Remember to 'oversew'

. . . .

(go forwards and backwards) at the end to ensure that the stitching doesn't come undone.

. . . .

10 Here the dog's body is being stitched with bold zigzag lines resembling fur. Use a straight stitch and the darning foot or free-machine-embroidery foot – this allows flexibility of movement.

10 Machine-stitching extra detail

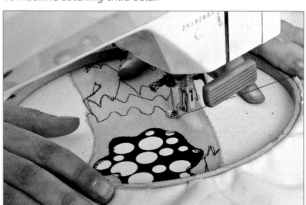

11 Stitching patterns with hand-sewing threads

12 Attaching buttons

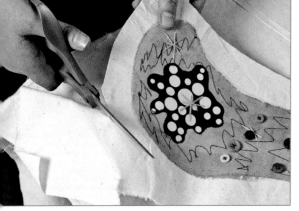

13 Cutting away excess fabric

14 Placing work on backing fabric

11 You can add extra decorative patterns, images and words. Here a large star shape is being created using hand-sewing thread.

12 You can also stitch on buttons, beads, washers, bells, and scraps of thin plastic.

TOP TIP

Make sure that any small items to be attached are not too large or heavy. Also, don't stitch them too close to the outside edges of the body parts, as these will be cut out later on.

13 Remove excess fabric by cutting all round each body part. Leave a large margin.

14 Place each body part on to the backing fabric of your choice.

TOP TIP

Felt is the easiest fabric to use for this particular type of backing. It doesn't fray, and it's easy to sew through and cut.

15 With the machine set to straight stitch, sew round the drawn edge, remembering to reverse and re-sew the last couple of stitches in order to secure them. When you have sewn round the edge of the body part, neatly cut through both layers leaving a 5 mm (1/4 in.) seam allowance (margin) all round.

15 Sewing through both layers

16 Edging with wool

16 To finish off each body part, the raw edge can be tidied and made stiffer by attaching thick wool, hand-sewing thread or pipe cleaners.

Use a zigzag stitch. Hold the wool or thread taut with one hand, and use the other hand to guide the fabric. Place the wool or thread close to the edge – try to follow your drawn outline – and slowly machine around the edge.

> ### TOP TIP
> *Don't rush it – go at a speed that you can easily control. Keep putting the needle in as you work your way round the edges.*

17 If you want to stick your crazy creatures to a backdrop – perhaps as a classroom wall hanging – it's best to use sticky-backed Velcro tabs. These allow you to mix and match body parts quickly and easily.

> ### TOP TIP
> *Before you stick on the Velcro tabs, put tiny pen marks on the back of each body part and on its desired location on the backdrop. This will help you get the tabs in the right positions.*

Crazy creatures can be added to a backdrop for classroom projects.

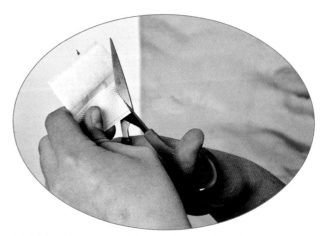

17 Adding sticky-backed Velcro tabs to each body part

Cut each Velcro tab to about 2 cm (³/₄ in.) long – they tend not to grip very well if you make them too small. Stick the 'hook' pads to each body part, and the fuzzy 'web' tabs to the backdrop.

7 wacky wings

This chapter focuses on layering different fabrics and weights of material, and removing or 'cutting through' layers to reveal the fabric below.

These techniques are great for encouraging children to be experimental, adapting materials and processes to explore various outcomes. There is no right or wrong way to combine fabrics, or to cut them so as to reveal what's underneath. If a child cuts through all the layers of fabric by accident, then they can simply place another layer behind and stitch around the shape again.

TECHNIQUES USED ....

* ❖ Making templates
* ❖ Cutting
* ❖ Sticking with iron-on web adhesive (Bondaweb)
* ❖ Machine- and hand-sewing

MATERIALS REQUIRED ....

* ❖ Cardboard
* ❖ Plain fabric or calico
* ❖ Selection of different fabrics – felts, plastics, chiffons, papers, etc.
* ❖ Pencils or fabric pens
* ❖ Fabric paints
* ❖ Beads, buttons
* ❖ Hand-sewing threads
* ❖ Thin wire or pipe cleaners
* ❖ Gaffer tape or duct tape

1 Tracing around the template

1 Create a cardboard wing template and draw round it onto plain fabric. To make a pair of wings, flip the template over and draw a second wing.

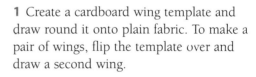

TOP TIP
Remember to create a generous point at the bottom end of the wing, where it will join the body – this is vital if you're going to attach the wings securely.

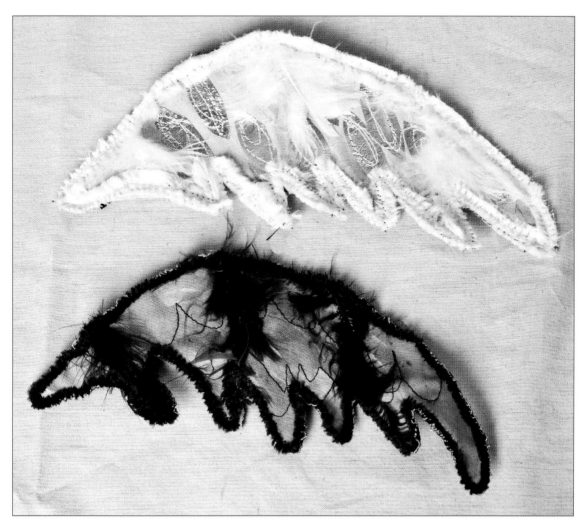

2 Using fabric paints and pens, fill in the wing design. Try mixing various colours together, or blending different colours to create a background effect.

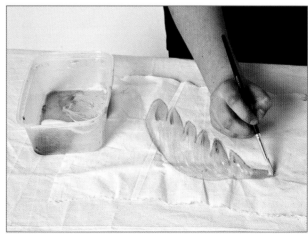

2 Filling in the wing design

3 Your wing designs can be as simple or as decorative as you like. These wings use fabric pens to create outlines and detail, with glitter paints to emphasise highlights.

4 When you have finished painting the background design, iron off to fix and dry the paint. If you want to make a very detailed design, remember to iron off at each stage so that the paint colours don't bleed together.

3 Examples of painted wing designs

4 Ironing off

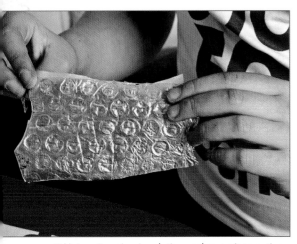

5 Hot-water-pipe insulation makes an interesting wing detail

5 Try adding texture and contrast to the wing by using appliqué images. Almost anything that you can stitch can be used – paper, foils, thin plastics or card, as well as lace and other decorative fabrics such as chiffon, velvet and felt.

> ## TOP TIP
> *You can sew into silver oven foil without tearing it by covering it in acetate or thin transparent plastic such as the kind used to make document wallets.*

6 The easiest way to attach appliqué detail to a wing is to use heat-bonded adhesive web (Bondaweb is the best known).

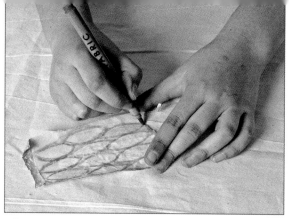

6 Drawing shapes onto backed appliqué material

7 Cutting out shapes for appliqué

The web is ironed onto the back of the material to be appliquéd. The paper backing of the web adhesive makes it easy to draw detailed designs, patterns or shapes.

> ### TOP TIP
> *Draw your shapes and patterns as close together as possible, like in a baking tray of biscuits. It's easier to cut them out and saves wasting the expensive web adhesive.*

7 Using small scissors, carefully cut out the shapes that will be appliquéd onto the wing.

8 Carefully peel the backing paper off each cut-out shape, and lay the shapes on the wing with the adhesive side downwards. Then very carefully place a clean piece of cloth over the wing, and iron gently to fix the appliqué shapes in place.

> ### TOP TIP
> *Take your time, especially when you put the cloth over the wing. Ask an adult to help with the ironing*

9 Heat-bonded web adhesive is not permanent. It holds work neatly and smoothly without the aid of pins, but for a lasting finish you need to stitch the appliqué shapes on to the wing.

8 Laying shapes on the wing, and ironing to heat-fix them

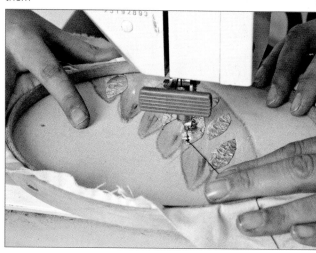

9 Stitching appliqué shapes to the wing

You can use either hand-stitching or machine-stitching. Here a small zigzag machine stitch allows the shape to be outlined and secured at the same time.

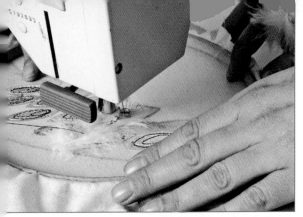

10 Adding feather decorations

11 Stiffening the wing using a pipe cleaner

12 Preparing layers for a multi-coloured cutwork wing

Of course, stitching can also be a decorative feature. You can use different types of stitch, different colours of thread, and different textures – for example, silk and wool.

· ·

10 Stitching small feathers onto the wing is just one way you can add extra interest and contrast. To attach a feather, use a zigzag stitch over the central quill of the feather.

You could also stitch on plastic fronds made from slashed plastic shopping bags, beads, ribbons, etc. – so let your imagination run wild!

11 If you want to attach your wings to a creature's body or a background picture, or you wish to wear your wings, you need to reinforce them so that they stand up. This wing is being stiffened with pipe cleaners, which are attached around the outer edge of the wing using a zigzag stitch. You can also use green garden wire, soft copper wire or drinking straws – the corrugated 'bendy' straws are ideal.

· ·

12 The first wing in this workshop used plain fabric, painted and decorated. This part of the workshop shows how to create decorative effects using layers, simple stitch and cutting through.

The wing illustrated uses three layers of different-coloured felts. Felt is an easy-to-use fabric – it doesn't stretch or fray, and it's easy to stitch and cut through. More experienced and confident children might like to try mixing and layering different materials – plastics, chiffons, velvets, silk, etc. – to give contrasts of weight and touch.

· ·

13 Use a wing template to trace out the wing outline on the top layer of fabric.

13 Drawing round the wing template

14 Stitching round the outline

TOP TIP
Remember to flip the template over to make a left-hand and right-hand pair of wings!

14 Set the machine to a straight stitch and sew all the way round the outline. Layers of felt need to be flat but don't need to be put into an embroidery ring – gentle hand pressure will keep the layers from moving while you stitch.

If you're using a mixture of materials, it's advisable to stretch them all tightly in an embroidery ring.

15 Drawing detail on the wings. This will be cut out.

15 Think of the cut-through wing as an advent calendar – you take away the top layers of material to reveal the hidden colours underneath. You can achieve this by cutting out small shapes from the wing. Draw simple shapes that are easy to sew round and cut out.

16 With the machine set to straight stitch, carefully sew round each of the drawn shapes.

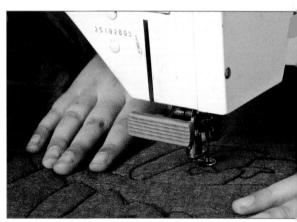

16 Sewing around the drawn shapes

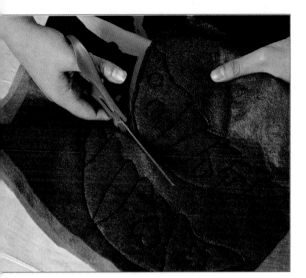

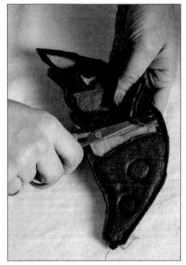

17 Cutting out the wings

18 Cutting through to reveal layers (1)

Cutting through to reveal layers (2)

17 Carefully cut around the outline of each wing, being sure to cut through all the layers together. If you're using felt, you don't need to leave a big margin of fabric, as the wing won't fray. Just leave a border along the line of the stitching, wide enough to stitch in a pipe cleaner for stiffening.

Other materials like velvet, hessian and denim tend to fray easily, so they need a border of at least 5 mm (¼ in.) before you can stitch in a pipe cleaner.

18 Carefully cut through one or more layers to reveal the different colours or textures underneath. In some areas of your design, you might want to cut through just one layer; in others, two layers. You could even experiment with cutting right through all the layers!

19 As in the first part of this workshop, reinforce the wing shape by stitching pipe cleaners around the outer edges.

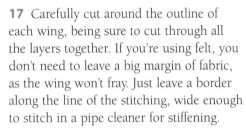

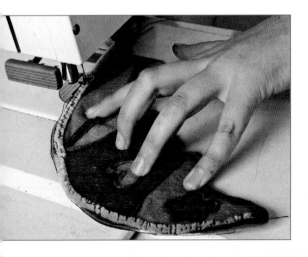

19 Stitching pipe cleaner to the edge of the wing

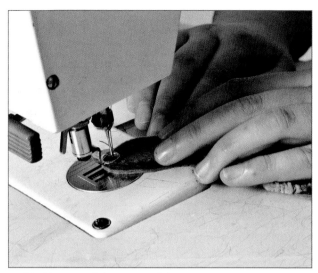

20 Stitching round the corner of the wing

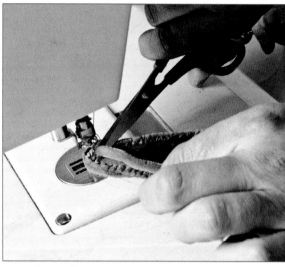

21 Finishing off

20 The trickiest part of attaching pipe cleaners is sewing round the corners of the wing. To make this easier, insert the needle and bend the pipe cleaner round the back of the needle, with the needle in the work.

21 Attach pipe cleaners all the way round the edges of the wing. When the two ends meet at the point where you started, lift up the foot with the needle inserted into the work, and trim away the excess pipe cleaner.

Put the foot back down, then sew forwards and backwards over the join to secure it.

8 brilliant butterfly

This chapter combines previously learned techniques – fabric painting, creating templates, decorating with pens and paints – with elements from other projects in this book (for example, the stiffened wings from the wacky wings project).

The butterfly incorporates both two-dimensional elements (wings) and a three-dimensional body, both of which can be embellished further with techniques such as appliqué, beading and hand and free-machine embroidery.

By this stage, children should have gained the confidence to mix and match techniques, processes and materials to create exciting and imaginative work that can be produced in manageable stages.

TECHNIQUES USED ·············

❖ Making templates for fabric cutting
❖ Fabric painting
❖ Decorating and beadwork
❖ Cutting
❖ Attaching wire to strengthen wings
❖ Creating pompoms
❖ Assembly of body parts

MATERIALS REQUIRED ··········

❖ Plain fabric
❖ Pencils or fabric pens
❖ Fabric paints
❖ Beads, buttons, hand-sewing threads
❖ Iron and ironing board
❖ Cardboard for creating templates
❖ Wool
❖ Scissors or shears
❖ Garden cane
❖ Thin wire or pipe cleaners
❖ Gaffer tape or duct tape

1 Creating the wing template

2 Cutting out the card template

1 Draw a simplified pattern of a wing shape onto card. Add an extra extension of 2 to 3 cm (¾ to 1⅛ in.) to the inside of the wing so that the wings can be sewn together where they will join the butterfly's body.

2 Cut out the card template, remembering to rotate the card around the scissors for easier cutting.

3 Carefully trace around the cardboard wing template onto the fabric. You will need two wings for each butterfly, so flip the template over to create a pair. The left and right wings will be mirror images, joined along the added extensions on their inside edges.

3 Tracing around the template onto fabric

4 Using fabric paint, fill in the wings. Try to blend colours to create bold, rich, highly decorative wings.

4 Painting the wing

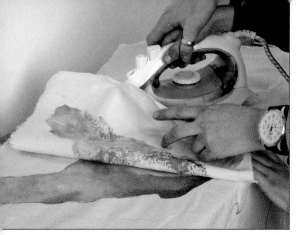

5 Ironing off

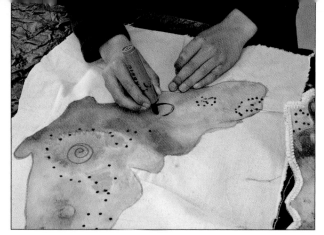

6 Decorating with fabric pens

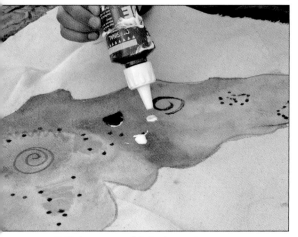

7 Gluing cut-up fabric decorations

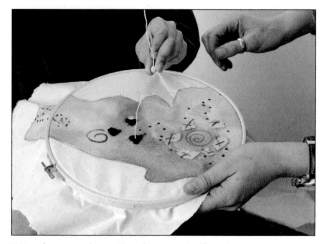

8 Hand-sewing decorative shapes onto the wing

5 Place a clean piece of fabric over each painted wing, and iron off to fix and dry the fabric paint.

6 Use fabric pens or crayons to add detail and depth to each wing.

7 Texture can be added with cut-up felts, fabrics, metallic foils, thin plastic sheets, slivers of CDs, etc. You could also print patterns onto and repeat images on the dried background colours. (See the Jungle Scene Project for ideas about printing and stencilling.)

8 Cut-out shapes can be secured using big hand-stitches. Experiment with bright or contrasting threads that will highlight the design.

9 Set up the sewing machine with the teeth up. Put a zigzag stitch foot on – despite its name, this can also be used for straight stitching. The zigzag foot is used here because you need a big zigzag stitch later to edge the wings with pipe cleaners.

9 The sewing-machine bed with the teeth up

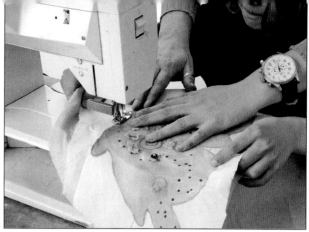

10 Attaching backing fabric

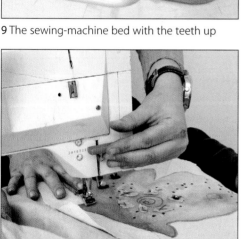

11 Lifting the presser foot bar

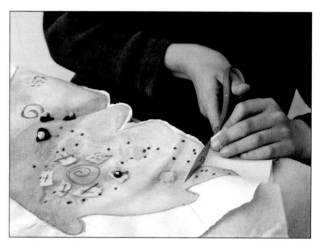

12 Cutting out

10 To give the wing extra weight, and to conceal the hand-sewing stitches and knots, place a piece of ironed medium-weight backing fabric behind it. Then stitch all around the wing shape.

It can be helpful for younger children if an adult uses their hand to keep the two pieces of fabric smooth on the bed of the sewing machine, and keeps the machine running at a manageable speed. Alternatively, the fabrics can be pinned together.

11 For straight or zigzag stitching, the presser foot keeps the fabric pressed tightly against the bed so that the fabric feeds smoothly.

TOP TIP

Insert the needle into the work so that you don't lose your place, and then lift the presser foot bar to release the pressure on the fabric. This allows you to turn the fabric to change the direction of stitching, making it much easier to follow curves and tight corners accurately.

12 Cut through both layers of the sewn wing, leaving a border of about 1 cm (⅜ in.).

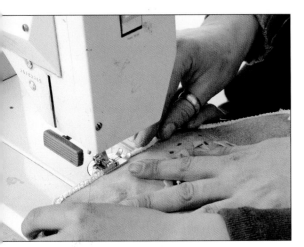

13 Edging with pipe cleaners

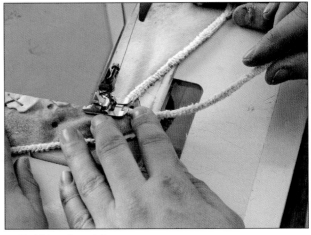

14 Finishing the edging

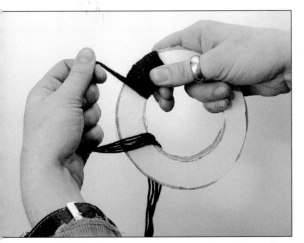

15 Winding wool on a pompom template

16 Tying off the wool

13 Place a pipe cleaner along the pre-sewn line. Using the widest zigzag setting, stitch over the pipe cleaner, following the edge of the work.

14 When you get near the end of a pipe cleaner, butt another up to it and continue to stitch over the join. When you have edged almost all the way round, trim the last pipe cleaner to the right length so that it butts up neatly to the first one.

Remember to reverse the direction of the stitch, or to oversew, to tie off the final zigzags.

15 Create two pompoms for the butterfly's head and body. You will need a big pompom for the body and a smaller one for the head. Draw circle ring templates onto stiff card. You need to cut two identical rings for each pompom. Wind wool tightly around the templates.

16 Tie off the wool once you have wound enough onto the template to create a big fluffy pompom ball.

17 Cutting through layers of wool   18 Opening out the pompom ball   19 Attaching the head to the body

17 Carefully cut through all layers of wool around the outer edge of the 'doughnut' shape.

· ·

18 Separate the two layers of card and tie a strand of wool tightly around the middle of the pompom ball. Then completely remove the layers of card.

· ·

19 Using a large-eyed needle, thread the wool and tie a knot at one end. Insert the needle right through the middle of the body pompom, and then through the head. Repeat this several times until the head is securely attached.

20 Attaching the 'feelers' (antennae)

· ·

20 Bend a pipe cleaner in half and attach it to the head at the centre point using several big stitches.

· ·

21 Loop one end of the pipe cleaner and sew through the loop several times.

21 Looping the pipe cleaner before attaching a pompom to the 'feeler' tip.

· ·

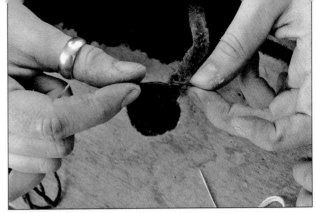

22 Stitching a tiny pompom to the end of a 'feeler'

23 Tying off a knot at the end of the 'feeler'

24 Overlapping the wing extensions

25 Stitching the wings together

22 Stitch through the middle of a tiny readymade pompom, large bead or polystyrene ball to attach it to the end of the pipe cleaner, creating the finished 'feeler'.

....

23 Don't forget to tie off knots when attaching pompoms to the ends of pipe cleaners.

24 Place the wings side by side along their flat edges. The extension on the top wing must completely overlap the one below.

....

25 Using large stitches, join the pair of wings together by sewing through them along the centre line.

....

26 Cut a piece of thin dowel or garden cane about 3 to 4 cm (1⅛ to 1½ in.) longer than the stitched centre line of the wings. (You might even find that you've got a pencil the right length.) Wiggle the wood through all the centre stitches and pull them tight. Don't knot or cut the wool – you'll be using it to attach the pompom body.

26 Inserting garden cane

• •

27 Joining the body and wings.

28 Securing the body to the 'backbone'.

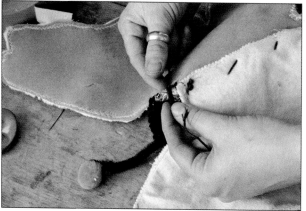
29 Tying off

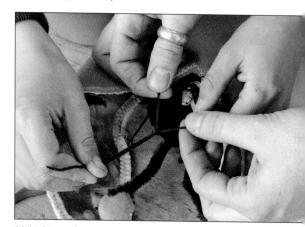
30 Making a loop

27 Using large stitches, go through the body and then stitch round the wooden 'backbone'. Attach the body all the way down the centre line of the wings.

. . . .

28 So that the body remains firmly attached to the 'backbone', wrap the wool around the stick as you progress.

. . . .

29 Make the ends of the cane safe by wrapping them in duct tape or gaffer tape. Then tie off securely.

. . . .

30 Tie the remaining wool to the top end of the 'backbone', to create a hanging loop.

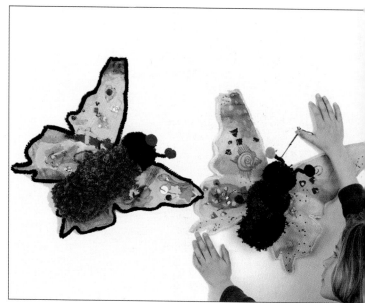
Finished butterflies

9 tiny tiger

This chapter shows how to transfer images from a flat two-dimensional design to a three-dimensional object.

TECHNIQUES USED ....

- ❧ Making templates for fabric cutting
- ❧ Fabric painting
- ❧ Attaching shapes to background with heat-fixing web
- ❧ Hand- and machine-stitching
- ❧ Cutting and pinning
- ❧ Decorating – beadwork
- ❧ Assembly of body parts

MATERIALS REQUIRED ....

- ❧ Plain fabric
- ❧ Fabric scraps (felt, patterned fabrics)
- ❧ Pencils or fabric pens, and fabric paints
- ❧ Beads, buttons, small dangling objects (e.g., keys, washers, paperclips)
- ❧ Hand- and machine-sewing threads
- ❧ Iron and ironing board
- ❧ Cardboard to create templates
- ❧ Wool, ribbon or string
- ❧ Scraps for stuffing (wool, paper, old socks, bubble wrap, etc.)
- ❧ Heat-fix adhesive web
- ❧ Pipe cleaner
- ❧ Scissors or shears
- ❧ Pins

1 Drawing head and body templates

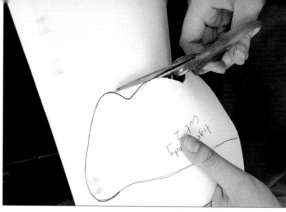

2 Cutting out the template shapes

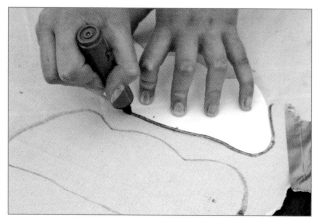

3 Tracing round the templates

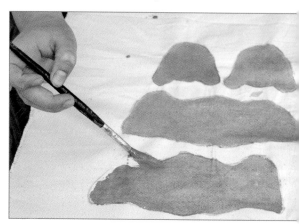

4 Painting the body shapes

You'll need a reference image of a tiger. This could be a child's drawing, a picture from a storybook, a cartoon still (for example, from *The Jungle Book*) or a photograph.

1 Work out the shapes of the tiger's head and body – keep them simple to make them easier to stitch and cut out. Draw the shapes on a piece of card. Don't worry about the legs and tail – you'll be making these later.

2 Cut out the card template shapes.

5 Cutting fabric for stripes

6 Positioning stripes, nose, eyes, etc.

3 Trace around the card template of the tiger's body to copy it onto a piece of plain fabric. An old pillowcase or sheet will do fine. You will need two shapes for each body part – a front panel and a back panel.

Repeat the process to make the front and back of the tiger's head.

7 Placing the work in an embroidery ring

4 Using fabric paint, fill in the shaped body parts to give the tiger his body colour. Then, when you've finished painting the tiger's body and head, remember to cover it with a clean cloth, and iron off to dry and fix the paint.

5 Choose fabrics to give the tiger his stripes, eyes, nose, etc. These can be rough or smooth, shiny, spotty, flowery, patterned – whatever! Iron on heat-fix web adhesive to the back of your chosen fabrics. Then draw simple shapes that are easy to cut out. Alternatively, you can cut out shapes and glue them to the tiger's body and head.

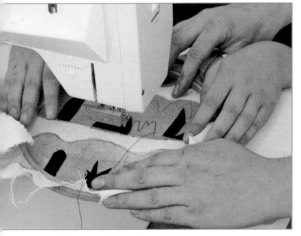

8 Free-machine stitching

6 Position the eyes, nose, mouth, stripes, etc. on the body parts, remembering that

9 Cutting out

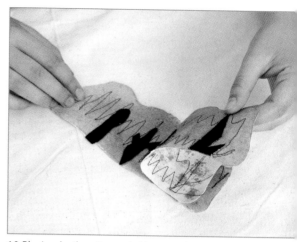

10 Placing both patterned sides together

you only need to decorate the front side of the tiger's head. If you have used heat-fix web, position the work on your ironing board, lay the fabric pieces on the body parts, then place a clean cloth over the work and iron off.

7 Set up the work in an embroidery ring as for machine-stitching. It's best to do this on a flat surface like your ironing board to get the work accurately placed and stretched tight.

8 Using free-machine stitching, set the dial to 'straight' or 'running' stitch. Then move the embroidery ring in large zigzag

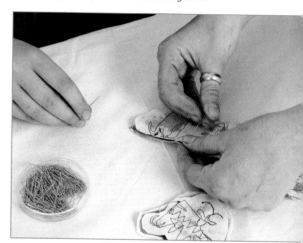

11 Pinning

patterns to create the look of fur. Keep your foot on the pedal at a steady speed, moving the ring towards you and away from you slowly. Keep the embroidery ring moving all the time the machine is running to avoid the thread clogging.

9 Cut out the embroidered body parts.

10 Place the two painted sides of the tiger's body together like a sandwich, so they lie exactly over each

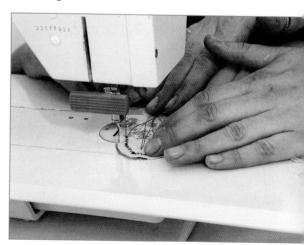

12 Sewing seams

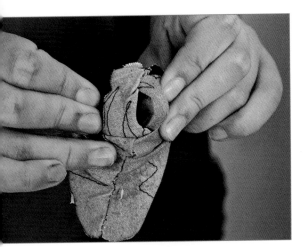

13 Turning work through

14 Stuffing

15 Stitching up the hole

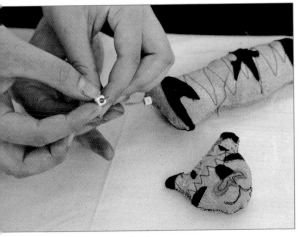

16 Decorating body parts

other. Do the same with the tiger's head.

11 Pin all the way round the tiger's body. Remember to leave a gap or seam allowance of 1 cm (⅜ in.) all the way round. Repeat the process for the tiger's head.

12 Set the machine to zigzag stitch and sew almost all the way round the edge of the tiger's body, leaving a gap of 4 cm to 5 cm (1½ to 2 in.). You need this size of gap so that you can turn the work through, ready for stuffing. Remember to oversew the stitches when you start and finish, so that they are tied off like a knot and don't unravel.

Repeat the process with the tiger's head.

13 Turn the tiger's body through so that you reveal the painted and decorated sides. It's just like turning a sock inside out! Do the same with the head.

14 You can use a variety of things for stuffing – old wool scraps, socks, bubble wrap, pieces of plastic foam, scrunched-up newspaper, tissues, little polystyrene beads, even lentils and small peas from the kitchen cupboard. Work the stuffing tightly into the body. A pencil, lolly stick or small spoon will help you to force the stuffing into the corners.

Repeat for the tiger's head.

. . . .

15 Using hand-sewing threads or wool, stitch up the hole.

. . . .

16 The tiger's body can be decorated in lots of ways. Using wool or thick thread, try making stitches through the body, tying a knot and then cutting both ends to leave strands. Buttons, beads, old bits of jewellery, etc. can all be attached by stitching through into the body.

17 When you've finished decorating the body, attach the head. Using big loops, sew into the body and then into the head,

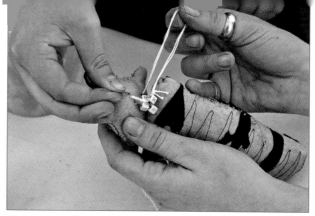
17 Attaching the head

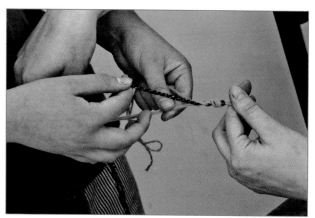
18 Making the legs

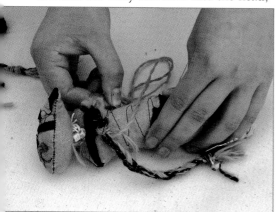
19 Attaching the legs to the body

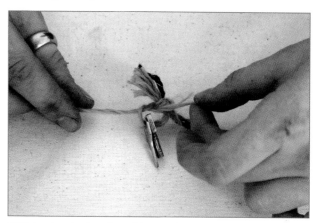
20 Tying jangly dangling objects to legs
21 Plaiting beads into a hanging loop

then pull tight. Repeat this several times until the head feels secure and doesn't flop about. Then tie off.

. . . .

. . . .

22 Attaching a hanging loop to the body

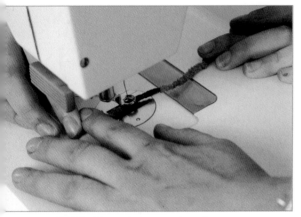

23 Stitching stripes onto the tail

24 Looping one end of the tail
25 Stitching the tail to the body

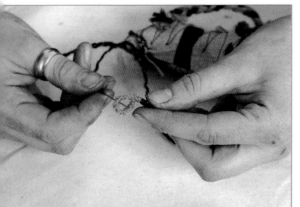

18 To make the tiger's legs, plait equal lengths of string, wool, ribbon, plastic strips, wire, drinking straws, raffia, etc. Then put a knot on each end so the plaits stay tight.

....

19 Stitch the legs onto the body with big tight loops, just like you did with the head.

....

20 To weight the legs so that they dangle, tie on small metal objects or beads. Things like keys, bells, paper clips and washers will make a lovely sound when the tiger is hanging.

21 A plaited hanging loop can be made in the same way as the legs. Try putting beads, shells, bells, etc. on individual strands and then plait them into the loop.

22 Knot each end of the hanging loop,

26 Two tiny tigers

....

other ideas for 3-D mobiles

Birds, fish, climbing monkeys, dinosaurs, horses, cats, bees, cars, Christmas trees…

10 sailing boat

This chapter is about constructing and building up a three-dimensional object from flat two-dimensional forms.

The boat form is simple enough for children to begin to grasp the idea of incorporating shapes and found objects in order to construct more complex designs. This workshop covers important everyday skills such as measuring, fitting and joining objects, combined with the more decorative textile techniques used to make and embellish the sails.

TECHNIQUES USED . . . .

❖ Making templates
❖ Selecting found objects for purpose
❖ Fitting and fixing – assembly of parts
❖ Cutting
❖ Gluing
❖ Painting
❖ Machine- and hand-sewing
❖ Wrapping with threads and wire

MATERIALS REQUIRED . . . .

❖ Cardboard
❖ Plain fabric
❖ Pencils or fabric pens
❖ Fabric paints
❖ Water-based or acrylic paints
❖ Beads, buttons
❖ Hand-sewing threads
❖ Thin wire
❖ Found objects: cotton reel, washers, old computer keys
❖ Garden cane
❖ Gaffer tape or duct tape

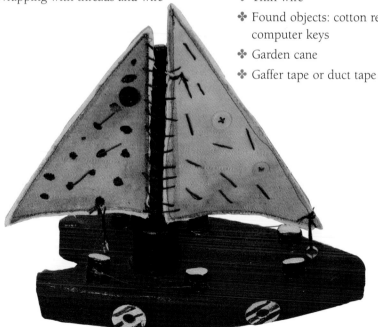

1 Draw a simple shape which will form the deck and bottom parts of the boat. You can draw freehand or use a found object – we used the flat 'sole' plate of an iron to trace around.

2 Cut out the boat shape and then trace around it to create an identical shape. Cut this out and you now have top (deck) and bottom (hull) pieces.

3 Decide how deep you want the sides of your boat to be. Then, using a straight edge or long ruler, draw a long line parallel to the edge of your piece of cardboard. When you cut it out, this strip of cardboard will be fixed between the top and bottom pieces of the boat, forming its sides.

1 Drawing the boat-deck shape

2 Tracing around the card template

TOP TIP

Measure the distance all the way around the edge of the boat hull with a piece of string. Your cardboard strip needs to be at least this length – add a few extra centimetres to be safe!

4 Cut along the line you've drawn to make a long thin strip of cardboard. It's important to keep it the same width all the way along.

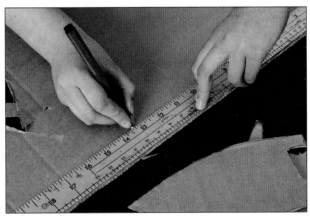

3 Marking off a long strip of card to form the side panels
4 Cutting out the cardboard strip

5 Hold the top piece of the boat shape against your body. With your other hand, take the strip and place its edge along the edge of the boat deck.

You'll find the next bit easier with a helper, who can cut small strips of tape and give them to you as you need them. Take your first piece of tape, place it neatly on the top piece of cardboard and press down firmly.

5 Taping the side strip to the top deck

6 Taping the bottom of the boat to the sides

7 Pasting newspaper strips to the boat shape
8 Painting a primer coat

Then smooth the overlapping tape over the join and fix smoothly onto the side piece. Repeat this process as you bend the cardboard strip to follow the shape of the boat.

It's easier to leave an overlap at the pointed 'bow' end of the boat. This can then be bent around the point and taped down on the other side to form a strong, neat join.

6 Turn the boat over and fit the bottom piece, taping it firmly as above.

7 To make the boat shape stronger and more durable, paste small strips of torn-up newspaper in layers over the cardboard. Use PVA or craft glue, allowing it to dry completely before painting.

8 To hide the newsprint and create a smooth surface, paint the boat shape with several coats of household emulsion or water-based craft paint, allowing it to dry before painting the top coat.

9 Choose small, regular-sized objects for the boat's bollards. We used keys from a broken computer keyboard, but cut-up pieces of cork, rubber or wood would all do the job fine.

Paint the bollards with emulsion.

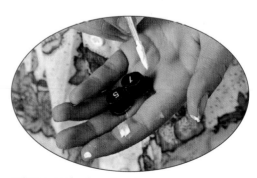

9 Computer keyboard parts

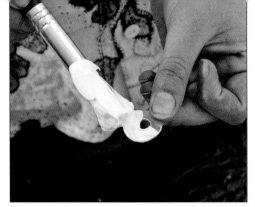
10 Painting washers

11 Painting a cotton reel for the mast foot

12 Painting the mast pole

13 Putting the finish coat on

10 Large washers have been chosen to make the boat's lifebelts. Small curtain rings, rubber tyres off broken toy vehicles or even Polo mints would all look good, too!

Whatever objects you choose, prime them by painting them with emulsion.

11 You need a rigid object into which to stick the mast pole. We've used a cotton reel, but a small matchbox or a child's building block with a hole drilled into it would work well. Whatever the object you choose, prime it by painting it with emulsion.

12 A piece of garden cane, a pencil or a paintbrush (with the brush end cut off) can be used to form the mast. Paint this with emulsion.

13 Choose your colour scheme for the boat, mast, bollards and lifebelts. Paint them all with a top coat of water-based or acrylic paint. Let them dry completely before assembly.

14 Finishing the fitting-out assembly

15 Inserting a small 'eye' screw

14 When all the parts are dry, you can 'fit out' your boat. Using PVA glue, stick the mast to the cotton reel, then stick the cotton reel to the deck of the boat. Attach the bollards around the edge of the deck at regular intervals. Stick the lifebelts to the sides of the boat.

When the glue on the bollards has dried completely, wrap thin wire, string or thick thread around them to join them all together – to create deck railings.

....

15 To hold the sails fast, you can fit a small 'eye' screw at either end of the boat. This will allow you to fasten a securing thread between the sail and the deck of the boat.

....

16 Planning and drawing the sails

16 The important thing to remember when planning the size of the sails is that the longest side needs to be a little bit shorter than the length of the mast – a ruler or set square will give you a neat, accurate shape that's the right size. The two sails don't have to be identical in design or size – but remember to make sure the long side (the side attached to the mast) is a straight line.

....

17 The sails can be made of plain cloth and painted with fabric paint, or made up from scrap material.

17 Painting the sails

18 If you're using fabric paint, iron off the background colour before adding painted detail.

18 Ironing off

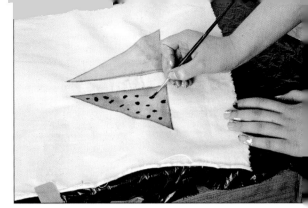

19 Adding detail to the sail

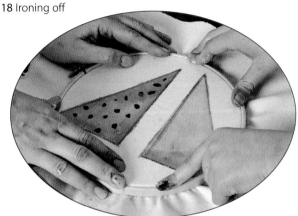

20 Putting the fabric into an embroidery ring

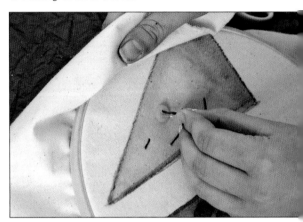

21 Adding buttons and bold hand-stitches

19 You can add detail to the sails with fabric paint, crayons or felt-tip pens. Your boat can be a pirate ship with a skull and crossbones on the sail, or decorated any other way you choose.

20 When you've finished painting or drawing on the sails, stretch the fabric tightly in an embroidery ring so that you can add hand-stitched detail.

21 The sails can be decorated with buttons, beads, big hand-stitches or appliqué designs.

22 Hand-stitching with thick threads adds interest and texture to the sails.

23 Once the sails have been decorated, remove the fabric from the embroidery ring. Then cut away the excess fabric, leaving an even margin of 2 to 3 cm (¾ to 1⅛ in.) around the sail.

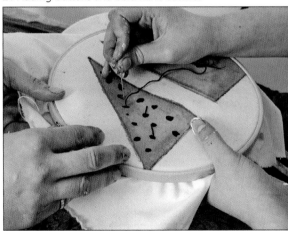

22 Hand-stitching detail into the sails
23 Cutting away excess fabric

24 Placing the sail on backing fabric

25 Stitching backing fabric to the sail

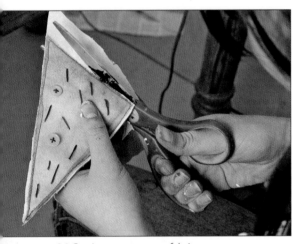

26 Cutting away excess fabric

27 Lacing the sail to the mast

24 To hide the messy stitching and knots on the back of the sails, use a backing fabric – this will also help to stiffen the sails. Lay the sail carefully over a piece of backing fabric cut to roughly the same size.

25 Using a straight stitch or zigzag foot, stitch around the edge of the sail design. The teeth need to be up for this task, so that the fabric is guided under the foot for easier stitching.

26 Once you have sewn all the way round the sail, reverse over the last couple of stitches to prevent it coming undone. Then carefully trim away the margin of fabric to leave a small seam allowance of about 2 mm (less than 1/8 in.) .

27 To attach the sail to the mast, knot a piece of hand-sewing thread and attach it to the top of the long edge of the sail. Then lace the sail to the mast with big hand-sewing stitches.

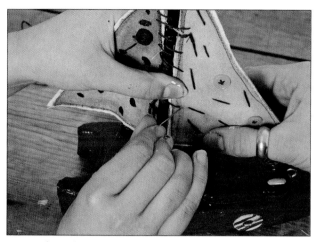

28 Attaching the second sail

29 Tying off the lacing

28 Repeat the lacing process to attach the second sail.

29 When both sails are firmly attached to the mast, tie off securely.

30 Attaching securing threads to the sail and eye

30 To finish the sails, knot a short length of hand-sewing thread and attach to the pointed corner of the sail nearest the metal 'eye' on the deck. Loop the thread through the eye, take up any slack thread and tie off.

The finished boat

⑪ starfish mobile

This workshop shows how objects can be created using stitch alone. The finished results are similar to traditional bobbin lace, but are achieved by using special 'boil away' water-soluble fabric.

Imaginative forms can be created using a mixture of media – threads, feathers, wires, fabrics – which are stitched onto the dissolvable fabric using free-machine and hand-embroidery techniques already learned. Once the backing fabric is immersed in water, it disappears, leaving the delicate, lacy 'skeleton' of the form behind.

Children find this process fascinating, and it lends itself to making leaves, spider webs, stars, flowers, birds and other lightweight designs that can be suspended – as in this seashore-inspired mobile. Alternatively, the finished shapes can be stitched onto screens, hangings, curtains, cushions, etc., or they can form pendants for earrings and other jewellery.

TECHNIQUES USED ·············

❖ Winding ribbon or other decorative coverings
❖ Freehand or template drawing and design
❖ Free-machine embroidery
❖ Hand embroidery
❖ Drilling objects
❖ Stiffening and wiring

MATERIALS REQUIRED ··········

❖ Willow, wire or embroidery ring for hanging frame
❖ Ribbon or thick wool
❖ PVA or craft glue
❖ Buttons, beads
❖ Seashells, pottery fragments, driftwood
❖ Water-soluble fabric
❖ Hand- and machine-sewing threads
❖ Embroidery ring

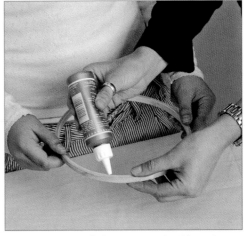

1 Putting a spot of glue on an embroidery ring

1 If you are using an embroidery ring to form the hanging frame, put a blob of PVA or craft glue on the rim so that you can attach the decorative ribbon or wool covering.

Alternatively, you can make a hanging frame from a loop of thin flexible hazel or willow, or from medium-weight wire (an old metal coat hanger is ideal).

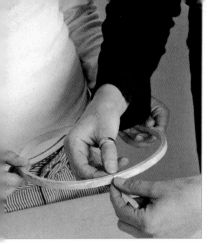
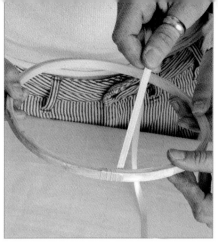
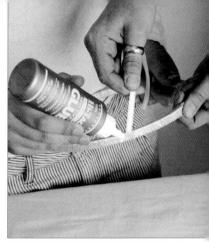

2 Glue the end of the ribbon to the frame and start wrapping

3 Winding on the ribbon and overlapping

4 Gluing the end of the ribbon

2 Glue the end of the ribbon or wool to the frame.

> ### TOP TIP
> *Put a pin at the beginning to hold the ribbon or wool firmly in place until the glue has dried.*

3 Wind the ribbon or wool tightly over the frame, overlapping it slightly.

> ### TOP TIP
> *Try mixing different types of ribbon or wool for added variety – or you could even use Christmas tinsel, coloured foil or plastic strips (e.g. cut-up carrier bags). You can also leave loose ends hanging as a decorative feature.*

4 It's a good idea to put a blob of glue every couple of inches around the frame so that the ribbon doesn't slip. When the hanging frame is covered, secure the loose end of the ribbon of wool with the blob of glue.

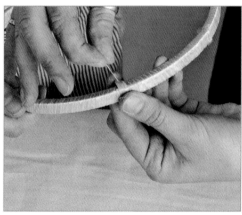

5 Pinning the ribbon

5 Remember to stick a pin in to hold the ribbon while the glue dries.

6 Use a diamond-tipped drill bit to make holes in shells, pottery or glass. Always set the piece of work in Plasticine, Play-Doh, Blu-Tack or putty to prevent it from moving or cracking. You'll probably need adult help with this.

7 Thread fine ribbon, wool, twine, fuse wire, fishing line, etc. through the holes you have drilled in the objects you've chosen as your hanging decorations. (As an alternative to drilling, you can secure objects by twisting soft copper wire around them.)

6 Drilling safely through the pot

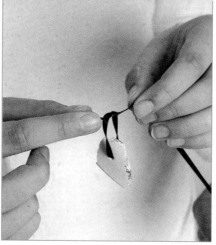
7 Tying on hanging decorations (1)

Tying on hanging decorations (2)

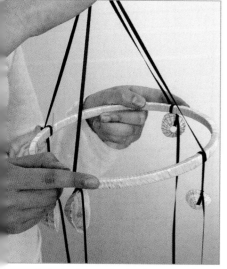
8 Gathering and tying hanging ribbons

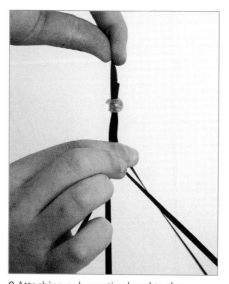
9 Attaching a decorative bead to the knotted ribbons

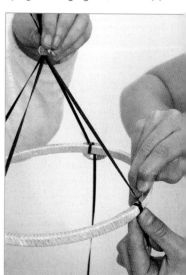
10 Pinning the ribbon to the frame

8 You need at least four hanging ribbons to make the mobile hang properly. It doesn't matter how many ribbons you use, but they must be tied to the frame at equal distances apart, otherwise the mobile will be lopsided.

Ask a helper to gather all the top ends of the ribbons together and knot them. With your helper holding both the frame and all the knotted ribbons at the top, wrap each individual hanging ribbon around the frame at an equal distance from its neighbours.

9 You can hide the knot at the top of the hanging ribbons by threading a large-eyed bead or any other object with a hole drilled through it.

10 Stick a pin in where each ribbon joins the frame. This holds the ribbon in place while you stitch it firmly and add further decoration. A quick fix is simply to tie a knot or put a blob of glue where the ribbon joins the frame.

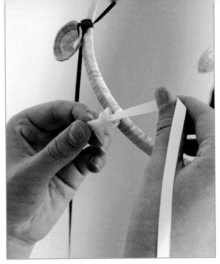

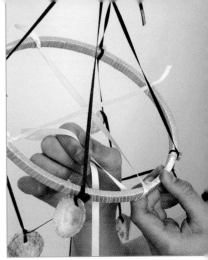

11 Attaching decorative detail

12 Tying a ribbon to the frame to create extra hanging supports

13 Criss-crossing the ribbons

11 You can stitch on buttons, beads, tiny seashells or little pompoms to add decorative detail.

12 By tying a ribbon across the hanging frame, you can create extra hanging supports.

13 The simplest way to fill the middle of the hanging frame is to criss-cross the ribbons in a regular pattern as in the picture above. You can also experiment with different geometrical shapes, such as stars and triangles.

14 If you tie the criss-cross ribbons together at the points where they cross, you can hang extra 'drops' or hanging ribbons from these points.

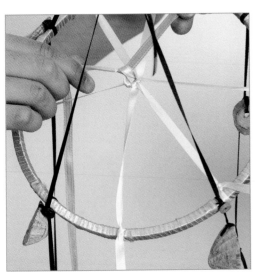

14 Tying the criss-cross ribbons together in the centre
15 Drawing starfish designs onto water-soluble fabric

15 Using a fabric pen, draw a selection of starfish shapes onto the water-soluble fabric. Position them close together (but not touching), a bit like biscuits on a baking tray. This means there is very little wastage of the expensive soluble fabric.

You are now ready to fill in the starfish shapes with free-machine embroidery. The stitches that you make now will be all that is left behind when the background fabric has been dissolved.

Be experimental – here are some techniques for creating interesting effects:

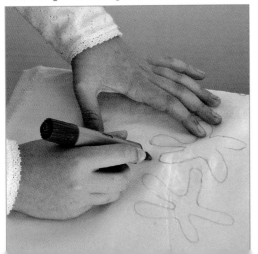

16 Winding hand-sewing thread onto bobbin

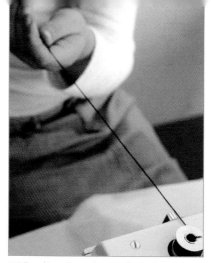

17 Feeding thread onto the bobbin under tension

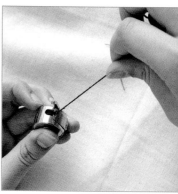

18 Positioning the the thread in the bobbin case

16 Put a thick thread on the bobbin. This gives a fantastic effect called 'free-machine couching', and looks like you have attached a thick thread by hand with lots of little stitches. In fact, you use the sewing machine to get a similar result much more quickly!

To load a bobbin with hand-sewing thread, first take several turns around the bobbin by hand, so that the thread grips. It doesn't matter whether you use an empty bobbin or one that already has some thread on it – as long as there is room for your extra hand-sewing thread on the bobbin.

17 When the end of the thread is secure, place the bobbin on the winder of the sewing machine. Keep hold of the hand-sewing thread, put your foot down on the foot control at a slow, even speed, and feed the thread onto the bobbin. Keep the thread under slight tension so that it winds evenly. Don't overfill the bobbin.

18 Pop the filled bobbin into its case, making sure the thread is guided correctly through the feed slot. If you are using a thick thread, you might need to loosen the tension on the bobbin case. To do this, turn the little screw on the bobbin case carefully, anticlockwise through one or two turns.

Once you feel confident with using a thick thread on your bobbin, try experimenting with a variety of different threads. Wool mixes, metallic threads and even glow-in-the-dark are all available from specialist suppliers. Using metallic threads can give spectacular results, although these are quite brittle and tend to break easily. To avoid this, put the metallic thread on the bobbin.

19 Set up the machine with your top and bottom thread, then fit a darning foot or free-machine embroidery foot. Remember to drop the teeth on the bed to allow you to move the work freely.

The soluble fabric must be stretched very tightly on an embroidery ring. Place the ring onto the bed of the machine, drop the presser foot, and then begin stitching.

19 Free-machining the starfish shapes

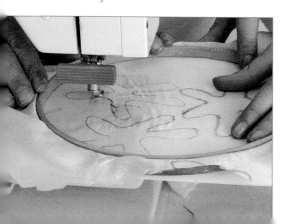

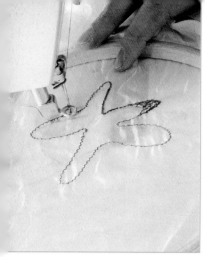

20 Outline stitching

21 Small pieces of fabric can be stitched into the work

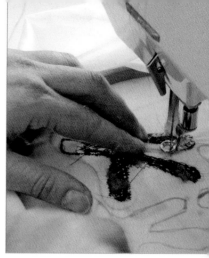

22 Stitching in pipe cleaners as stiffening material

A small child will find it easier to move the ring and fill in the starfish shape with stitches. Think of it as a bit like scribbling and shading in a drawing. Don't worry if you go outside the edges of the design – the final shape can be trimmed later.

20 Children who are more confident with machine-stitching can follow the outline of the shape with zigzag stitches and then fill in.

21 For added texture and interest, try cutting up scraps of fabric, thin plastic sheet, textured wool, etc. and adding them to the design at random. As you stitch, these scraps will be caught and securely attached.

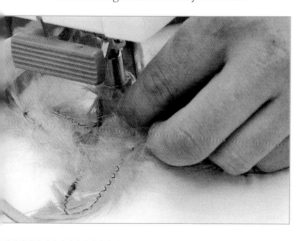

22 Using a zigzag stitch set at the widest possible setting, lay a pipe cleaner on the outline edge of the shape. Carefully stitch over the pipe cleaner, turning the ring as you follow the curves in the shape (as in the butterfly project).

This technique strengthens the shape and ensures that it doesn't distort when the backing fabric has dissolved.

23 Another interesting variation is to stitch feathers around the edge of the shape. Use a zigzag stitch (as with the pipe cleaner above) and stitch over the flexible shaft of the feather. The feather can be bent to follow the shape of the design, and one feather can be butted up to another and trimmed off.

24 When all the stitching has been completed, remove the ring and trim away all the excess fabric.

25 Dissolvable fabric can either be hot- or cold-water soluble, so read the instructions carefully. Cold-water-soluble fabrics simply need soaking in a basin.

23 Sewing feathers into the shape

24 Cutting away excess fabric

25 Dissolving the fabric in a kettle

26 Ironing off the shapes to flatten and dry them

For safety reasons, hot-water-soluble fabric is best dissolved in a kettle – so adult supervision is essential! When the fabric has boiled away, to avoid scalds tip the water plus the shapes into a sink half full of cold water. Then fish out the shapes and place them on a clean cloth.

26 Place a clean cloth on top of the work and iron off carefully. This will dry the shapes and flatten them at the same time.

A selection of delicate starfishes ready for hanging

27 Stitch or knot the finished starfish shapes to the hanging ribbons.

27 Attaching a starfish to a length of ribbon

12 happy hats

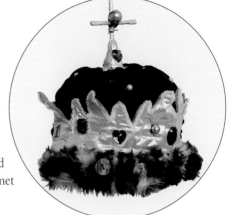

This chapter combines many of the techniques already demonstrated to produce three different types of hat: a simple dinosaur cap, a helmet inspired by Roman armour, and regal jewelled crowns.

These three designs are intended to spark off other creative ideas for headgear, costumes and accessories. Fairy tiaras, wizards' and witches' hats, spacemen's helmets, sci-fi creatures and animal heads are just a few of the items to which the techniques in this chapter could be adapted.

TECHNIQUES USED • • • • • • • • • • •

❖ Creating templates
❖ Beading and embellishment
❖ Creating 3-D forms with shirring elastic
❖ Stuffing
❖ Attaching and pinning
❖ Wiring and stiffening
❖ Papier mâché forms
❖ Free-machine embroidery

MATERIALS REQUIRED • • • • • • • • •

❖ Swimming cap
❖ Shirring elastic
❖ Embroidery rings of various sizes
❖ Hand and machine threads
❖ Buttons, beads, pompoms, decorative embellishments
❖ Lightweight fabric for shirring
❖ Wadding or old socks for stuffing
❖ Newspaper, PVA glue for papier mâché
❖ Balloon(s)
❖ Pipe cleaners
❖ Fur for trimming, or velvet, or metallic fabrics or foils
❖ Boiler/radiator insulation ('bubble' type)
❖ Acrylic paints
❖ Empty bobbin reels
❖ Feathers
❖ Baby's dummy/bottle teat
❖ Fine dowel

1st project • dinosaur hat

First find or draw some pictures of dinosaurs that will help you design the shapes for your dinosaur cap – horns, spikes, scales or whatever you like.

1 You'll need a Lycra swimming cap – this fabric is easier to work than the old-style rubber or latex swimming caps. It's also more comfortable to wear!

2 Mark out several circles on the cap, spacing them equally.

3 Set the machine to a small zigzag stitch and sew round each circle that you have marked on the cap. You might find it easier to secure the cap material in a small embroidery ring to keep the fabric stretched taut while you sew.

1 A swimming cap

2 Drawing circles on the cap

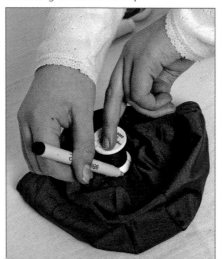

3 Zigzag stitching round the circle

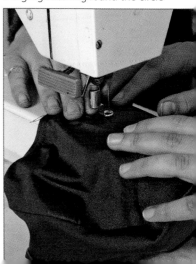

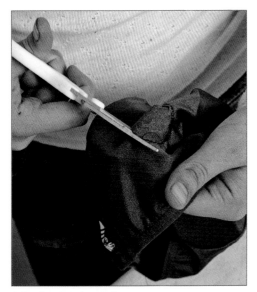

4 Cutting out the circles

4 Cut out each circle, cutting carefully inside each stitch line. The stitches contain the circle and make it easier to insert the dinosaur 'spikes'.

5 Start winding the shirring elastic onto a bobbin by hand, wrapping it several times around the bobbin in a clockwise direction. Put the bobbin onto the machine's thread winder, then gently put your foot on the pedal. Taking the elastic thread in your hand as shown here will add tension, ensuring that the elastic is wound tightly onto the bobbin.

6 Put the filled bobbin into the bobbin case. Guide the elastic thread as you would with normal sewing thread.

7 Select a lightweight fabric to create the dinosaur 'spikes'. The lighter the fabric's weight, the more 'gathered' the effect when you sew in the shirring elastic.

8 Thread the machine with normal machine thread on the top, and set it to a straight stitch. Start sewing from the centre of the embroidery ring, working in an ever-increasing circle to produce a spiral.

5 Winding the shirring elastic onto a bobbin

6 Threading the shirring elastic through the shuttle case

The thread in the correct position in the guide

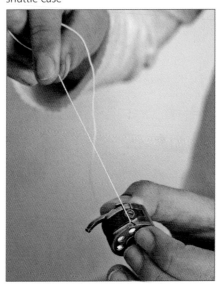

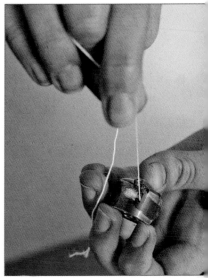

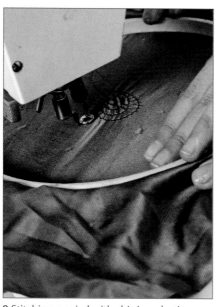

7 Put the fabric into an embroidery ring

8 Stitching a spiral with shirring elastic on the bobbin

Finishing the spiral

The closer and tighter you make the spiral shape, the more it will 'gather' into a conical pointed shape.

Remember to oversew (as in tying a knot) when you start and finish the spiral.

Experiment with different weights of fabric and different sizes of spiral to create the effect you want for the dinosaur's spikes. The bigger the spiral, the bigger the spike!

Pop the fabric out of the embroidery ring.

· ·

9 When the stitched spiral is released from the embroidery ring, trim away the excess fabric. Leave a seam allowance of about 2 cm (¾ in.).

· ·

10 Stuff the conical spike with wadding, scraps of wool or fabric, or old socks.

9 Cutting away the 'spike'
10 Stuffing the spike

· ·

93

11 Placing the spike on the backing fabric

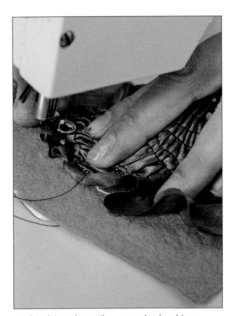

12 Stitching the spike onto the backing fabric

13 Trimming the spike

11 Place the firmly stuffed spike onto a backing fabric – felt is ideal as it has a bit of 'give', is easy to work with and doesn't fray.

12 Set the machine to a small zigzag. Sew carefully around the bottom of the spike, using the outer stitch line as a guide.

13 Trim off the excess fabric and backing, leaving a small seam allowance of about 1 cm (⅜ in.).

14 When you have made as many spikes as there are holes in the cap, push one spike at a time through each hole, ready to be attached to the cap.

15 With the machine set to a small zigzag stitch, sew through the cap around the original circular stitch line.

Remember to oversew at the beginning and end to secure your stitches.

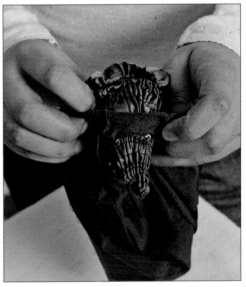

14 Pushing the spike through the cap

TOP TIP

Holding the tip of the spike in the palm of your hand as you sew round will prevent it getting caught under the machine's foot.

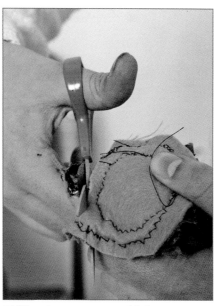

15 Stitching the spike to the cap   16 Trimming away excess fabric   17 Adding more spikes.

16 With the cap turned inside out, hold the cap and spike firmly in one hand, then trim away any excess fabric from the bottom of each spike.

17 Repeat the sequence until all the spikes have been secured to the cap.

Your dinosaur cap can be used in the swimming pool or even in the bath!

The finished cap

2nd project • regal crowns

First find some reference pictures to give you an idea of what sort of crown you would like to design.

1 Draw two parallel lines on paper or thin card. The distance you choose between the lines will be the depth of the crown.

2 When you've drawn your lines the right length, measure the middle point on each line and mark it.

TOP TIP

Measure round your head above your ears and brow with a piece of string or a tape measure. Your lines need to be about 2 cm (¾ in.) longer than the measurement around your head.

1 Drawing parallel guide lines.

2 Marking the middle

3 Drawing the template for the points on the crown

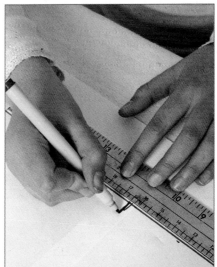

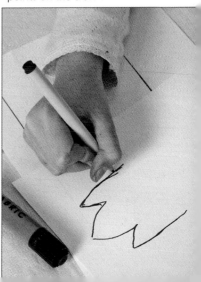

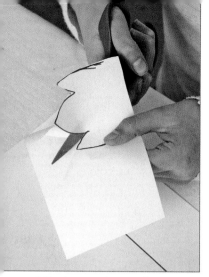

4 Cutting out the template

5 Placing the template on the middle of the card strip

6 Tracing repeat shapes

3 To create the points around the top rim of the crown, draw a simple template shape.

. . . .

4 Cut out the template shape.

. . . .

5 Position the template at the midpoint of your drawn line.

. . . .

6 Trace the outline of the pointed shape at the midpoint first, then repeat until you have an evenly spaced crown template. Cut out the template shape, with a straight line at the bottom and the detailed crown patterns at the top.

. . . .

7 Choose the fabric material for the surface of the crown. Here we are using a silver metallic fabric, but you can also try using foil-backed plastics such as radiator or boiler insulation material, or silver foil encased in clear plastic.

Select a stiff interfacing material for the middle layer, between the surface fabric and the lining. This gives the crown stiffness and weight. Here we have used a thick felt, but you could try heavy blotting paper or iron-on interfacing from a haberdashery shop.

The lining will be next to your head, so it needs to be soft. Felt is ideal as it doesn't fray and is easy to work with.

Layer the three fabrics together.

. . . .

8 Place the cut-out template on the top layer of the fabric and trace around the design.

● ●

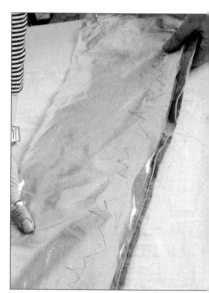

7 Layering three fabrics
8 Transferring the template shape to the fabric

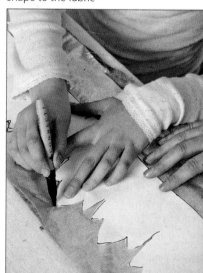

9 Sewing around the template shape

10 Cutting out the crown shape

11 Edging the crown with pipe cleaners

9 Sew along the lines of the pattern. You can use free-machine embroidery if you are able to follow the line confidently. Alternatively, put the teeth up on the machine, fit the standard zigzag/straight-stitch foot, and follow the lines.

10 Carefully cut out the crown shape, following the stitch lines closely with a very small allowance of perhaps 2 mm (less than 1/8 in.).

11 Using a wide zigzag stitch, place a pipe cleaner on the stitch line and attach. Butt a new pipe cleaner up when you're near the end of the first pipe cleaner and continue stitching. Repeat this process until the top edge and sides of the crown have been stiffened.

12 Joining the edges to form the crown ring

12 Fold the fabric strip so that the outer ('right') side faces inwards and the lining is on the outside. Pin the two edges together to form a ring of fabric like a big headband – this is the body of the crown.

13 Stitching the edge seam

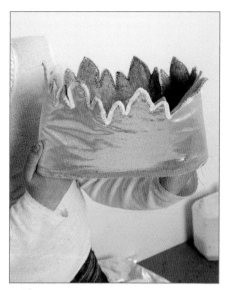

14 The crown ring

15 Using an iron to turn up
the edges of trim

13 With the machine set on straight stitch,
sew along the seam edge.

14 Turn the work through so that the 'right'
side is on the outside. This is your crown
ring ready to be decorated.

If you want to trim your crown with fake fur,
ribbon or braid, cut a strip of your chosen
fabric a little bit longer than the circumference of your crown.

15 Your trim will be easier to stitch if you
turn up the edges top and bottom. Iron
them firmly in place.

16 Turn the crown ring inside out
17 Pinning the trim to the crown ring

16 Turn the crown ring inside out.

17 Place the furry side of the trim (the
'right' side) against the lining of the crown
ring at the bottom edge of the headband. Pin
it neatly.

18 Sewing on the trim

19 Bringing together the ends of the trim to form a seam

20 Sewing the joining seam of the trim band

18 With a straight stitch set and teeth up using a standard foot, sew over the pins to attach the trim to the crown ring.

19 Where the beginning of the trim strip meets the end, put the two furry sides together to form a seam. Pin in position.

21 Trimming away any excess trim

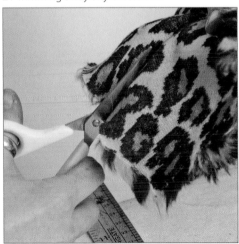

20 With the machine setting on straight stitch and the teeth up, sew along the seam line. Remember to oversew at the beginning and the end.

21 Cut away any excess trim fabric to leave a seam allowance of about 1.5 cm (⅝ in.).

22 Turn up the trim material around the circumference of the crown, pinning it evenly in position.

22 Turning up the trim and pinning it in position

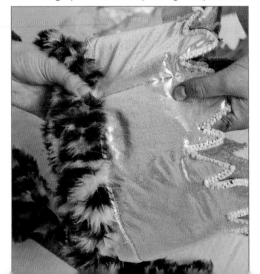

23 Sewing the trim around the crown

24 Decorating with a small pompom

Embellishing with a button

23 With the machine set to straight stitch, sew along the top edge of the trim to secure it.

· ·

24 The trim band and crown can be decorated with all sorts of small objects – buttons, beads, pompoms, stick-on felts or jewels, washers, thick silver foil (e.g. milk-bottle tops)… the choices are endless!

Using stick-on jewels

25 The finished crown – quite regal enough for most kings or queens! But to give it even more splendour, read on…

25 The finished crown

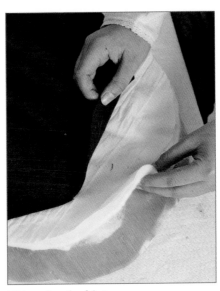

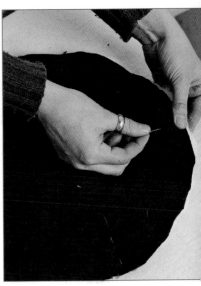

26 Cutting fabric for a cap to fit inside the crown

27 Layering the fabrics

28 Pinning the layers

26 To make the crown even more impressive, you can create a sumptuous gathered cap to fit inside it. This can also support an orb or a jewelled headpiece.

Use a large plate or pan lid as a template for the cap. The larger the fabric circle, the more gathered you can make the cap.

Choose a thick, rich material such as velvet or brocade, which can be gathered easily but is not too heavy to sew through. Cut out a large circle of fabric for the surface of the cap, then select a lightweight fabric for a lining and also some scrap material such as an old duvet or wadding to give extra thickness and softness – this will go between the top layer and the lining.

27 Cut circles of the same size as the top layer. Lay them on top of each other like a sandwich, ready to pin.

28 Pin the three layers at equal distances around the outside of the circle.

29 Measure and cut a strip of fabric to make the sides of the cap that will be attached to the inside of the crown. This can be the same fabric as the top of the cap (as shown), though most of it will be hidden inside the crown, so don't worry if you decide to use another sort of material.

Your strip needs to be the same length as the circumference of the crown. The depth is not critical but should be at least 5 cm (2 in.) – enough to hold the base of the cap so that it can be sewn inside the crown.

29 Cutting a fabric strip for the cap sides

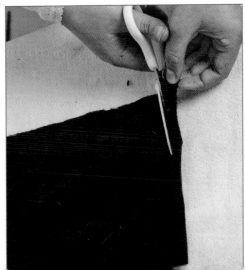

30 Sewing the layers together

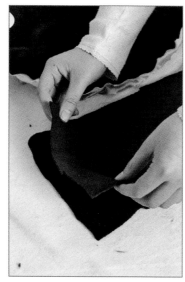

31 Joining the fabric strip

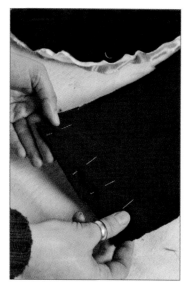

32 Pinning the seam

30 Put shirring elastic on the bobbin (as in the dinosaur hat workshop) and run a line of elastic all the way round the circle. This gathers the fabrics together like a mop cap.

31 Turn the fabric strip on itself, 'right' sides together, and bring the two short edges together to form a joining seam.

32 Pin the seam, with the pins horizontal to the cut edge.

33 With the machine set to straight stitch, sew over the joining seam. Remember to overstitch at each end.

34 Turn the cap band inside out so that the seam is on the outside.

35 Take the cap circle with the 'right' side (the surface that will be seen when the crown is finished) facing downwards. Then pin the outside edge of the gathered circle to the edge of the cap band, with both 'right' edges facing each other.

33 Sewing the joining seam

34 Turning the cap band inside out

35 Pinning the cap inside the cap band

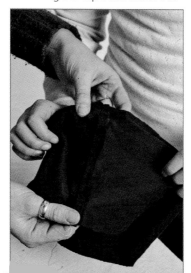

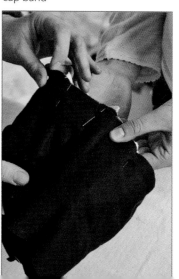

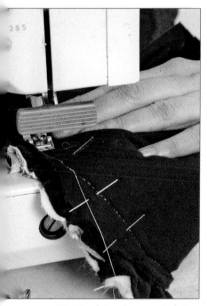

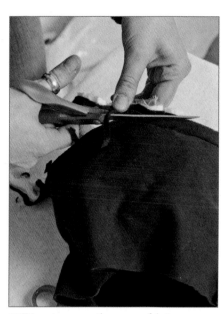

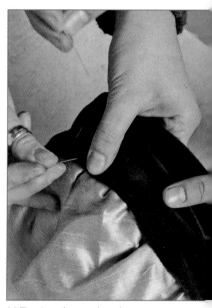

36 Attaching the cap circle to the cap band

37 Trimming away the excess fabric

38 Turning the cap band

36 With the machine set on straight stitch and the teeth up, sew through all the layers to attach the cap circle to the cap band.

....

37 Carefully cut away any excess fabric, leaving a seam allowance of 1.5 cm (⅝ in.).

....

38 With the cap turned inside out and the lining material on view, turn up the band so that the edge of it overlaps and covers the stitch line. Then pin it in position.

39 With the machine set to straight stitch, sew over the pins to attach the turned-up cap band.

....

40 Turn the cap the right way out. Using big stitches, gather the excess fabric. It helps to insert the needle through about 5 mm (¼ in.) of fabric, then turn the needle anticlockwise about half a turn, put the needle back through the fabric, and finally come up and pull tight. This bunches the fabric into a decorative 'gather'.

39 Sewing the turned-up cap band

40 Gathering the cap

Attaching a decorative bead

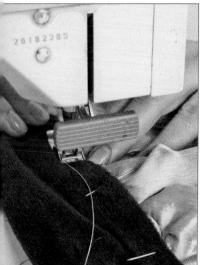

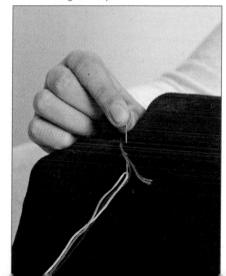

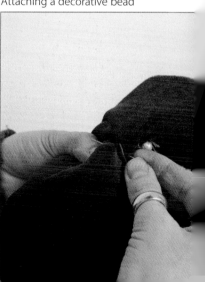

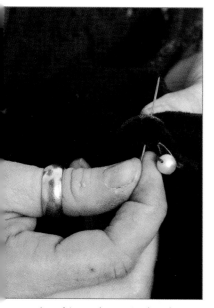

Attaching a decorative bead

41 The cap being placed inside the crown

42 Attaching the cap to the crown ring

If you like, at the same time you can also sew on a bead or button to hide the stitches. Alternatively, try making a feature of the stitches by using a contrasting thread.

41 Position the cap so that it sits inside the upper part of the crown ring. Try to keep the bottom edge of the cap band neatly butted up to the top edge of the trim band.

42 Using hand stitches inserted every 5 cm (2 in.) or so, attach the cap to the crown ring. Make sure you sew through all the layers of material.

43 Cutting the tip off a bottle teat

43 A final flourish to top off your regal creation is a finial or cross. This can be formed using a variety of household objects – a detergent-bottle nozzle, an empty bobbin, a rolled-up cardboard cone, or (as shown) a baby's feeding-bottle teat.

Cut a small hole in the top of the teat.

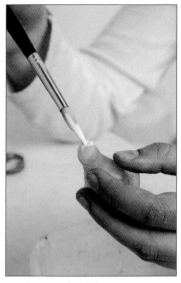  

44 Gluing to hold the cross in position

45 Inserting a small dowel or lollipop stick

46 Wrapping the cross with strips of pasted newspaper

44 Put a blob of PVA glue in the hole you have made.

45 Insert a short length of thin dowel or a lollipop stick. This will form the vertical part of the cross or finial.

46 Cut a shorter length of dowel for the horizontal crosspiece. Then wrap thinly torn strips of newspaper dipped in PVA to secure the crosspiece to the vertical. Continue wrapping.

47 Once the cross has been completely covered in papier mâché, allow it to dry overnight before painting.

48 Paint the cross with metallic gold or silver paint.

47 The cross ready for painting

48 Painting the cross

 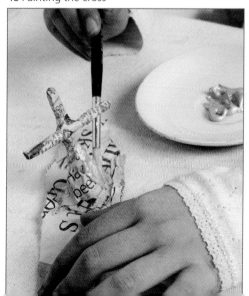

49 Attaching the cross finial

49 Trim away the excess papier mâché around the base of the cross finial, following the shape of the bottom of the teat.

To attach the finial to the crown cap, make a big stitch or a knot on the top middle of the cap. Sew through the rubber into the crown, back and forth until the finial is attached all around its base. Then tie off securely.

Fit for a queen: the finished crown

As a final touch, you might like to sew a big jewel or pearl onto the cross.

....

50 Instead of putting a cross finial on your crown, you could try making stiffened or wired supports, sewn into the inside of the crown band and then tied together at their top ends. Here we have used the same silver fabric as the body of the crown, stiffened with pipe cleaners. We also used yellow pipe cleaners to stiffen the top edge of the crown, adding contrast and colour.

50 A variation on the crown

3rd project • legionnaire's helmet

Find some reference pictures of ancient helmets. We chose to design a Roman legionnaire's helmet.

1 Blow up a party balloon. Tear up some strips of newspaper. Spread PVA glue onto the balloon, covering it from the bottom to about halfway up. This will form the cap part of the helmet.

Glue on several layers of newspaper strips. This makes the body of the helmet stronger.

Leave to dry at least overnight, and the longer the better.

1 Inflate a balloon and glue on some paper strips

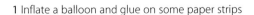

2 The helmet form

3 Shaping the helmet

4 Cutting away the excess papier mâché

2 When the papier mâché is dry, pop the balloon and remove the balloon rubber from the inside of the helmet.

3 Place the roughly shaped helmet form on the wearer's head and mark where the ears will be.

4 With a sharp pair of scissors, cut away the excess papier mâché over the ears.

5 Make a slit up from the bottom edge of the helmet form, about 10 to 12 cm (4 to 5 in.) long. This will allow you to fit the helmet closely to the wearer's head by overlapping any excess papier mâché.

6 Put the helmet on the wearer's head and adjust it to the right size. Secure the overlapped papier mâché with a piece of duct tape.

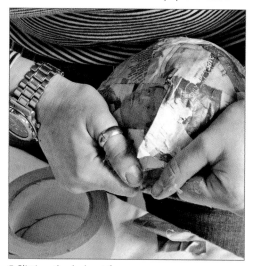

5 Slitting the helmet form
6 Taping up the fitted helmet

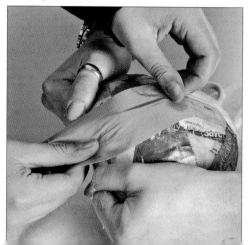

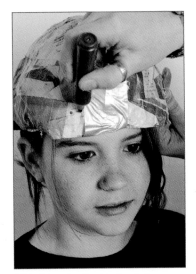

7 Marking the final helmet shape

8 Creating 3-D patterns using pipe cleaners

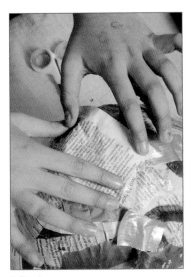

9 Pasting paper over pipe cleaners

7 With the helmet on the wearer's head, mark round the rim to form an even edge. It helps if the front of the helmet is higher than the back – it will sit on the head more securely and comfortably.

8 You can add texture to the surface of the helmet by taping pipe cleaners, heavy wire or cable in a pattern on the helmet's surface. When this is covered and painted, it will look like decorated metal.

10 Squeezing the papier mâché over the 3-D form

11 The finished helmet form ready for decoration

9 Build up another couple of layers of papier mâché to cover the three-dimensional material that you have used to create the patterned surface.

10 To make the three-dimensional form underneath the papier mâché stand out and create a strong pattern, squeeze or

pinch the paper tightly over the form while the glue is still wet.

11 Let the papier mâché dry out overnight; then your finished and fitted helmet form is ready to paint and decorate.

12 Priming the helmet form

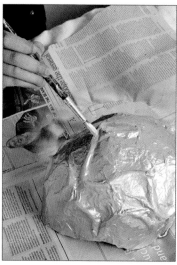

13 Applying the silver topcoat

14 Gluing an empty bobbin

12 Using thick emulsion paint, give the helmet several coats to achieve an even surface. Here we've used white emulsion paint because we intend to finish with a silver topcoat to look like metal. However, the Romans also wore black, red and gold-coloured helmets, so you can use darker undercoats if you plan to use a dark topcoat.

13 Use a silver metallic paint for the topcoat. It is safer to use acrylic paint or radiator paint, not specialist car paints which give off toxic fumes. If there is an adult helper, you could use spray paint as an alternative. Always follow the instructions on the paint can or aerosol container carefully.

14 To make a base for the upright feather plumes on the top of the helmet, we decided to glue empty bobbins in a row across the helmet, though matchboxes or corks would do just as well.

15 The bobbins should be stuck in a straight line from the middle of the front of the helmet to the centre of the back.

15 Sticking the bobbin to the helmet

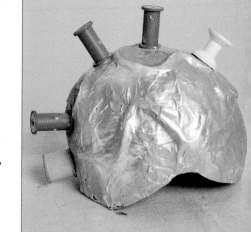

The helmet with plume supports in place

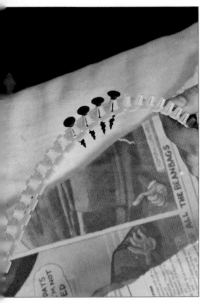

16 A plastic strip to hold the feather quills

17 Gluing the feather quills

Inserting quills into the securing strip

16 You need to find something to form a strip that will hold the quills of the feather plume in position. We've used the empty plastic belt from a nail, screw or rivet gun, but you could also use a strip of thick corrugated card or several layers of duct tape folded into a stiff strip. Bear in mind that you'll need to make holes at equal intervals along the strip if you are using cardboard or plastic.

....

17 Dip the quill part of the feathers into PVA glue. You don't have to use feathers – twisted bundles of raffia, paper spills, Scoubi Dous or even thin twisted electrical wires will all give interesting effects.

....

18 Wrap the strip to which the feathers are secured in duct tape. Wrapping the tape around the strip and turning it in gives an extra width which helps when attaching it to the bobbins.

18 Attaching feather plumes to the helmet

19 Securing one end of the strip

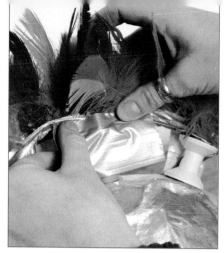

20 Taping up the sides of the plume strip

21 The taped-up plume strip

22 Sticking papier mâché to the plume base

23 Coating with PVA glue

24 Priming with emulsion paint

19 Use duct tape to secure each section of the plume strip to each bobbin.

20 When all the bobbins are fixed to the plume strip, fill in the gaps between the bobbins with tape.

21 Tape along both sides of the plume strip until the bobbins and gaps are completely covered.

22 Glue strips of torn newspaper over the tape to create a surface for painting.

23 Using a thick brush dipped in the PVA glue, cover the plume base to smooth down all the torn edges and give a smooth surface for painting. Leave to dry.

24 Carefully prime the plume base with emulsion paint, taking care not to get any paint on the feathers. Allow to dry thoroughly, then finish with a topcoat of the paint of your choice. We've used silver to match the body of the helmet.

25 Cutting a template for the brow piece

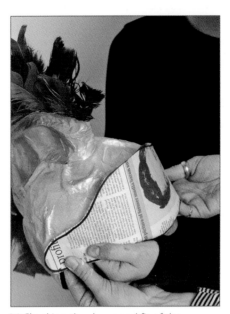

26 Checking the shape and fit of the brow template

27 Transferring the template to fabric

25 To create the brow piece over the front of the helmet, first measure the front part of the helmet from ear to ear. Then decide how deep you want your brow piece and draw a template shape on card or paper. Cut this out.

26 Before you transfer the design to fabric, check what the brow piece will look like and how well it fits. Simply hold it in place against the helmet, then mark off any area to be removed or reshaped.

27 Place the template on the fabric of your choice. We have used a silver-foil-backed boiler-insulation material. You might like to use a metallic fabric or even thin plastic sheet.

28 Doubling up the layers
29 Draw a template for the cheek pieces

28 Place the roughly trimmed fabric with the template shape on top of a scrap of the same material or on a backing fabric. This will give it stiffness.

29 Create the template for the two cheek pieces. You only need one template, but remember to flip it over after you have traced one shape onto the fabric – this will give you symmetrical left and right cheek pieces.

30 Sewing a pattern into the cheek piece

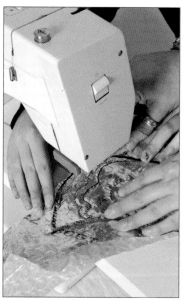

31 Edging with pipe cleaners

Sewing in pipe cleaners

30 With the free-machine embroidery foot fitted and the teeth down, you can create a pattern on each cheek piece. Sewing into the middle of a piece before you edge it will help to keep the fabric flat and prevent it from puckering up.

31 With the stitch set to large zigzag, hold a pipe cleaner along the outer line of the cheek piece and stitch in place. Remember to butt each pipe cleaner up against the last one as you go along, and trim off any extra length when you join up at the point you started at.

32 Trim away any excess fabric around the outside of the pipe cleaners. You don't need a seam allowance but do be careful not to cut through the stitches!

TOP TIP
Put the work into an embroidery ring if you find it easier to control when using free-machine stitching.

32 Removing excess fabric

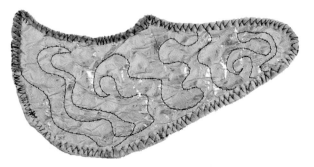
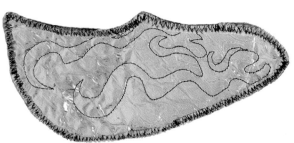

The finished cheek pieces ready to be attached

33 Instead of using stitch lines to decorate the brow piece, you could try using pipe cleaners, coloured string or bright wire stitched into place. You still need to use pipe cleaners to give the brow piece a stiff edge.

· ·

34 You will need to create holes with a sharp skewer or screwdriver to attach the cheek and brow pieces to the helmet. Ask an adult for help if you need it. It's safest to push through the fabric into a soft material – not your hand! We've used a piece of polystyrene.

35 Position the cheek and brow pieces in the desired places on the helmet, and mark off where you need to make holes in both the helmet and the fabric pieces. The two holes in the helmet should be slightly above and just in front of your ears. You should make these holes using a large screw and a screwdriver.

· ·

36 Position the cheek piece under the brow piece; then line up the two holes in the fabric with the hole in the helmet. Use a metal paper fastener, pushing it carefully through the two pieces one layer at a time and then through the helmet.

33 Decorating and stiffening the brow piece with pipe cleaner

34 Making a hole in the top of the cheek piece

35 Making holes in the helmet

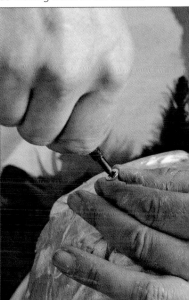

36 Lining up the holes before fastening the prongs

37 Splay the prongs of the fastener to secure

38 Taping over the prongs

37 With your thumb pressed down firmly on the head of the paper fastener, spread the two prongs of the fastener and press them down flat against the inside of the helmet.

38 So that the prongs of the fastener don't rub against the wearer's head, cover them with a couple of squares of duct tape or more layers of papier mâché.

The same fabric, stitching and edging could be used to create gauntlets and protective arm and leg pieces similar to those a real Roman legionary would have worn.

The finished helmet

illustrated glossary

ADHESIVES ············

Adhesives can be used in textile work as an alternative to stitching.

PVA or special textile adhesive can be used to stick one fabric surface to another

RIGHT Heat-fixed web adhesive is ironed onto the back of the fabric to be attached (top); then the protective paper backing is peeled off (right). Finally, the web-backed fabric is ironed onto the fabric below

APPLIQUÉ ·····································

A French word that basically means attaching one piece of fabric on top of another. The attachment can be made by either hand-sewing, machine-stitching or even gluing.

The appliqué design is usually cut out and then attached to background objects. This technique has a huge number of variations giving different decorative effects.

RIGHT Using appliqué detail in the Tiny Tiger workshop

'BOIL-AWAY' FABRIC – SEE WATER-SOLUBLE FABRIC

CUTWORK

Cutwork is usually achieved by stitching together layers of fabric of different weights and colours, and then cutting away one or more layers to reveal the contrasting colours, textures and patterns beneath. Always take care to stitch outlines around the shapes to be cut away – this prevents fraying.

Cutwork exposes different layers of fabric to give extra depth

EMBROIDERY RING

This holds the work taut to allow easier free-machining or hand-sewing. Rings can be made of wood, plastic or metal.

For free-machining, put the ring with the adjustable screw on the bottom, then the fabric and then the other half of the ring, and pull the fabric tight, as if it were a drumskin. For hand-sewing, have the adjustable screw on top.

When using a ring with very fine work, or where the ring will mark the fabric (such as with the pile on a velvet), the ring can be bound with fabric to prevent this happening.

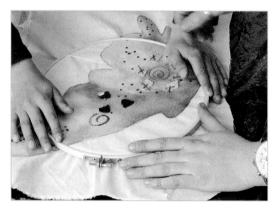

RIGHT Fabric held tightly in an embroidery ring to allow easier free-machine stitching

LEFT Embroidery ring with the screw on top for hand-sewing

FABRICS

Woven fabrics can be split into two types: natural (cotton, silk, calico, linen, wool, hessian) and man-made or synthetic (polyesters, rayons, acetates, viscose, acrylics). There are also many fibre mixes – poly/cotton is the most common – as well as mixes which incorporate stretch materials such as Lycra and jersey. And there are non-woven fabrics such as felt and leather, as well as laminated fabrics.

Different weights and textures of fabric

Certain fabrics can be either natural or man-made – silks, velvets, laces and chiffons, for example. Surface textures can be decorative (for example, printing, stencilling, flocking, devoré, moiré, embossing) or functional (cording, waterproofing, fire retardant, etc.).

It's a great idea to pick up fabric scraps whenever you see them – bits of worn-out clothes, leftovers from upholstery or curtain-making, interesting packaging.

TOP TIP

Keep your fabrics sorted in bags according to purpose and type – for example, leathers and furs together, denims and canvas together, silks with chiffons, etc.

FABRIC PENS, CRAYONS & MARKERS

Special pens and markers for drawing, outlining and adding detail on fabrics (they also work on paper, card, etc). Sometimes sold as 'T-shirt markers'; different types are available for use on other fabrics. Can be fixed with heat to give permanent results (see IRONING OFF).

Fabric pens

FOUND OBJECTS

Natural or man-made items that can be added to a piece as decoration (for example, shells, broken pottery). Also objects that can be used as templates for shapes and patterns (for example, dishes, mugs, glasses, building blocks).

Some found objects also make great printing blocks or stencils – see the Jungle Scene workshop for some ideas.

LEFT Found objects like these can be used to trace shapes for your designs

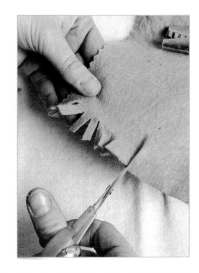

FRINGING

Decorative edging effect produced by cutting or slashing the outer edge of a piece of fabric.

Fringing the edge of a piece of felt

IRONING OFF

Drying and fixing fabric paint by means of heat. Cover the work with a clean cloth. With the iron set on 'high', hold in place for a couple of seconds. The top cloth will absorb excess paint as well as protecting the work below.

Ironing off with a clean cloth over the work dries and fixes colours

NEEDLES

Needles come in different thicknesses and lengths depending on purpose.

Machine needles vary slightly in design according to machine type. Always select a machine needle of the correct size and point for the fabric and thread you choose. The smaller the number on the needle, the finer it is: Size 70 is a very fine needle used for lightweight fabrics. Bigger numbers denote coarser needles for heavier fabrics.

The needle is held in place by the needle clamp. This can be loosened off with the clamp screw to remove a needle, then tightened up after a new needle has been inserted into the clamp.

Hand-sewing needles come in a wide range of lengths and thicknesses. For general hand-sewing, these are usually 'sharps', which are medium length and suitable for almost all fabric weights. Embroidery needles tend to have a larger eye. Tapestry needles are thicker and blunter, with a big eye suitable for wools and thick threads.

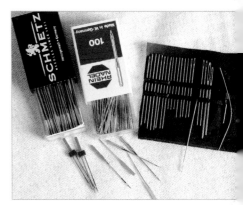

A selection of machine needles (left) and hand-sewing needles (right)

PAINTS

Acrylic A water-based plastic paint that is thick and gives strong solid colours. It is not ideal for use on fabric as it sits on the surface and tends to flake off if fabric is folded or sewn into. But acrylic is ideal for painting wood, paper, card, etc.

Gouache A water-based paint, sometimes also called tempera. It is semi-opaque, allowing tones to be created by using thin washes in layers. Suitable for painting heavier fabrics such as canvas. Unsuitable for any applications where the finished work needs to be washed.

Poster Inexpensive water-based paint, available either ready-mixed or as powder colours. Good for covering large areas of paper or card quickly and cheaply – for instance, for backdrops.

Acrylic paint gives solid colours. It is good for painting wood, card and papier mâché

A selection of specialist fabric paints

Fabric paint Most fabric paints are water-based. All are wash-resistant after they have been fixed using heat (see IRONING OFF). Gloss, 'bright', glitter, pearl and metallic paints are available, and these can be mixed to give a wide variety of effects. Fabric paint sticks are also available – these are more like wax crayons to use.

PAPIER MÂCHÉ

Torn-paper/glue mixture that can be built up in layers to create a durable form. Classic papier mâché is newsprint and wallpaper paste, mulched up and applied in layers. Variants include screwing up dried newspaper and then using masking tape to create the form, then adding the mulch. Alternatively, use strips of newspaper, each dipped in PVA glue and smoothed over a form.

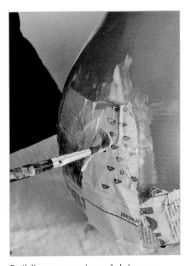

Building up papier mâché on a balloon to form a headpiece

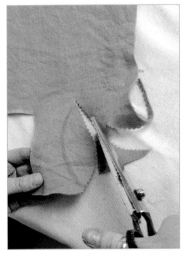

Cutting a shape with zigzag 'pinked' edges using pinking shears

PINKING

This is the name given to the tooth-like zigzag edge produced by special scissors called pinking shears. Pinking is both decorative and functional – the pinked edges prevent the work from fraying.

POMPOMS

Larger pompoms can be made by wrapping wool around a cardboard ring and then cutting away. They can be used to create bodies for creatures (see the Brilliant Butterfly workshop). Smaller pompoms can be bought from haberdashers or craft shops; these are generally used decoratively, stitched into work or stuck on.

Winding wool to create a large pompom

PRIMER/PRIMING ·······

A base coat of paint to seal the surface of paper, wood, fabric, etc.

SEAM ALLOWANCE ······

The border or margin left outside the stitch line. Leaving a seam allowance prevents fraying. It can also be a decorative feature. A small seam allowance is also used so that decorative or reinforcing edging can be added.

Using a thick coat of primer to seal a papier mâché form

Trimming to leave a small seam allowance

STITCHES ··································

Machine embroidery The term for any stitch produced by a sewing machine. The most commonly used stitches are 'running' and 'zigzag' stitches, which are basic dressmaking stitches. These use the presser foot and have the teeth up, enabling the fabric to be guided through the machine. The weight of the presser foot can be adjusted depending on the weight of the fabric. These simple machine stitches are used for outlining, attaching and seaming. A short stitch length makes it easier to manoeuvre the presser foot around curves.

Preset or programmed stitch patterns are available on most sewing machines.

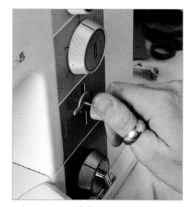

Adjusting stitch length

Free-machine-embroidery foot (or darning foot) with the teeth up

Free-machine-embroidery foot (or darning foot) with the teeth down

Adjusting stitch width

Free-machine embroidery is a more creative technique that allows the user to 'draw' with the thread. The machine's teeth or feed must be able to be dropped into the bed or covered, so that the fabric is not gripped. This can be done by lifting a lever to lower the teeth or using a cover plate. Instead of the teeth gripping the fabric, you are in complete control of the direction in which you stitch. You can move the work up, down, sideways and around the needle – or in any combination. It's a bit like drawing with a pencil.

It is easier to free-machine embroider if work is placed in an embroidery ring. This sits on the bed of the machine and can be moved around the needle freely.

For the projects in this book, we have used a free-machine-embroidery foot. The foot is an important safety feature that shields the needle: do not remove it when working with children!

Some experienced textile artists prefer to free-machine embroider without using a foot. This is only possible if the fabric is stretched really tight, and if the work is not too layered, thick or bulky.

Free-machine embroidery using a straight stitch

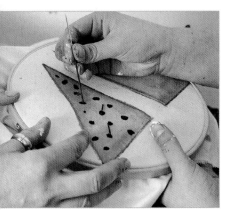

Decorative hand-stitching using an embroidery ring

Hand-stitching can be functional or decorative. In its functional role, it is used for attaching fasteners such as zips, buttons or Velcro; or for joining two seams; or for attaching components together. In its decorative role, hand stitching can be used to work in thick threads or even wire. It can be used to attach beads, sequins, and found objects such as shells, twigs or pierced pottery fragments.

Free-machine embroidery using a zigzag stitch

STUFFING ·····························

A flat object made up of two or more panels stitched together can be turned into a three-dimensional object by using stuffing to fill out the form. Stuffing can be wadding or kapok, cut-up woollen scraps, old socks or tights. In general, if you are trying to create a lightweight object, use kapok or fabrics that will not be too bulky.

Stuffing the body of a toy using knitted scraps

TAPING

Strong flexible tapes such as duct tape or gaffer tape are useful for attaching objects such as car or wood, and holding them in position. Tapes can also be used in layers to build up strength.

TEMPLATE

A shape or pattern made of card, plastic sheet or cloth which is used to make duplicate shapes.

Taping

THREADS

Threads come in almost as many varieties as fabrics. They are made of different types of yarn (polyesters, cottons, wools, silks, mixes) and are available in a huge range of colours.

Hand-sewing threads tend to be thicker, with more strands than machine thread. Some even have metallic strands twisted into them. Hand-sewing threads usually come loosely wound on reels or in skeins or hanks.

Most machine threads come tightly wound on a spool or bobbin – this ensures that the tension remains constant when the yarn is threaded onto a sewing machine. They come in different weights – a 30 is suitable for heavier fabrics, a 60 is lighter.

Always try to choose the right thread for the purpose – a heavy fabric will tend to need a heavier thread, while silks and chiffons need a very lightweight thread.

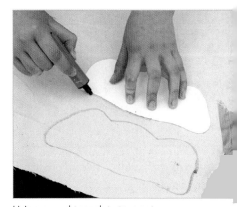

Using a card template to create identical shapes for construction

A selection of hand-sewing threads (left) and machine threads (right)

TYING OFF ....

Prevents stitches coming undone. To tie off by hand, make a knot or several small stitches in the same place, and then cut the thread (but not too close to the knot!)

Using a machine, go forwards and backwards over the same part of the work – this is called oversewing.

WATER-SOLUBLE FABRIC ....

A specialist type of fabric that can be stitched decoratively with threads and wires, then dissolved away using either hot or cold water. Hot-water-soluble fabric is sometimes called 'boil-away' because it can be dissolved in a kettle.

Hot-water-soluble fabric can be 'boiled away'

index

OUCHY COLLEGE
LIBRARY